You're a
Natural
Champion

Sound Wisdom Books by Zig Ziglar

A View from the Top

A View from the Top Action Guide

Goals

ZIG ZIGLAR

You're a Natural Champion

ALLOW YOUR SELF-ESTEEM & POSITIVE MINDSET TO SHINE

Published and distributed by:
SOUND WISDOM
P.O. Box 310
Shippensburg, PA 17257-0310
717-530-2122

info@soundwisdom.com

www.soundwisdom.com

Cover/jacket designer: Eileen Rockwell

ISBN 13 TP: 978-1-64095-092-4

ISBN 13 eBook: 978-1-64095-093-1

For Worldwide Distribution, Printed in the U.S.A.

1 2 3 4 5 6 7 8 / 24 23 22 21 20

Contents

Introduction

Since the beginning of time, there never has been and there never will be another person just like you. You're rare. You're unique. You're different. You were designed for accomplishment. You're engineered for success. You're endowed with the seeds of greatness.

But the question is, do you feel this way? Do you believe you can accomplish anything you set out to do? Or have you found that success always eludes you? If so, you need to readjust your thinking and reshape your attitudes. You need to visualize yourself as a success. In short, you need to repaint your self-image and Zig Ziglar will show you how.

Through this book, we at Nightingale-Conant invite you to join Zig to learn, from the master himself, the secrets of cultivating a successful self-image. Zig has been through it all from his early days as a struggling cookware salesman to becoming one of the country's foremost motivational speakers—helping millions to realize their potential. Zig Ziglar is the personification of the healthy self-image.

As he puts it, "The elements usually conducive to high self-esteem are good family relationships, good moral standards, religion, close friends, financial well-being, hobbies, and status." But how many people have all these elements or even some of them? Are you going to take a backseat and let the world pass you by? Will you let a low self-image stand in the way of success and the realization of your goals? You won't have to if you change the way you see yourself.

It all begins when you start believing in you and having faith in your abilities. It culminates when you realize that you can have anything you want if you help enough people get what they want. This simple little truth has worked for others and it will work for you. You'll find that you can build and nurture your self-esteem, inspire others, and enjoy success you never dreamed possible.

It's all within your reach because, *"You can change what you are. You can change where you are by changing what goes into your mind."*

Zig Ziglar grew a one-man sales company to a corporation. His books have sold millions of copies and have been translated into several languages. And that's no wonder because what Zig Ziglar says stems from a deep personal experience and from proven professional success.

Motivation and positive thinking won't work for the individual who does not believe that they themselves are capable of doing anything.

So start now to strengthen your belief in yourself and your abilities as you read this book—you will become a proud achiever with a successful self-image that shouts, "I can!"

CHAPTER 1

How You See Yourself

Just for a moment, let's play a little game. It's early in the morning. Your telephone rings, the voice at the other end says, "Hello friend, I've been meaning to call you for a long time. You know, I think you're one of the nicest people I've ever met in my life. You're a real asset to the community. You're a credit to your profession. What a delight it is to be able to call you friend. You know, I wish that you and I could spend more time together because every time I'm with you, I'm so much more enthusiastic. I do so much better.

"And you know what else, if I could spend twenty minutes a day with you, my life would be wonderfully rich, and I could do so much more. I know I should have called you and told you this years ago, but for whatever reason, I didn't do it and I just wanted to do it now. I look forward to the next time I see you and we can spend some time together. See you later."

And he hangs up.

Now let me ask you a question. If you ever received such a telephone call as that, or if you should get such a phone call as that and it was from an old and trusted friend, and you knew he was deadly serious, let me ask you, "What kind of day would you have?" It would be magnificent, wouldn't it?

If you were a doctor, would you be a better doctor? If you were a household executive, would you be a better household executive? If you were going on a sales call, would you make a better, more effective sales call? Would you be a better mother? Would you be a better truck driver? Would you be a better student? Would you be better at whatever it is that you're doing? Do you believe you would be better at whatever you do?

Now, how much more would you know about being a doctor, or a truck driver, or a household executive, or a salesperson? You wouldn't know any more, but you would be substantially better because all of a sudden your image has changed. Your attitude has changed. Why? Because you're thinking, *I'm an asset to my community. I'm a credit to my profession. That friend said so and he's one smart cookie.* I mean, you wouldn't argue with that at all, would you?

The truth is you would feel better, do better, and be better because you would think a little more of yourself.

Now since that would make you feel so much better, let me ask you a question: Why don't you make a phone call like that on a regular basis to someone whom you know and respect and admire, whom you could honestly say something nice about? Your call would surely make that person's day better.

I have a good friend who is also a speaker, a very prominent one. He heard me go through this little routine one day, and he said, "You know, I think I'm going to give that a shot." The following Saturday night he phoned a friend of his whom he had not seen in a few weeks. And when he started the conversation similar to that one just mentioned, maybe not quite that flowery, but saying something really nice, the man at the other end was so shocked and so excited and so enthused, that they spent about thirty minutes talking.

My friend said that when he put the telephone down, he felt higher than a kite. And so consequently, every Saturday night he makes a call to someone.

I believe firmly that you can have everything in life you want—if you help enough other people get what they want. But you've got to understand that is a concept. That it is a philosophy—not a tactic. If you do it with the thought that, *I'm going to do this for you and I expect you to do something for me,* it does not work.

The reason this concept works both for the recipient and the one who places the call is that it follows a good basic human relationship principle. The need to feel important has been described as the most important function in our life. And unless we can be, on occasion, made to feel important, we're not going to be functioning at our best. As we look at self-image throughout this book, that's exactly what we are talking about—a telephone call that you receive or you make will make you feel better. It will do something positive for your self-image.

I believe firmly that you can have everything in life you want—if you help enough other people get what they want.

THREE THIEVES

Now, how important is your image? Dr. Joyce Brothers says that the way you dress, the occupation you choose, the mate you select, the moral conduct, and all these things are tied to the picture we have of ourselves. It is true that we cannot perform in a manner that is inconsistent with the way we see ourselves.

Therefore, I'd like to tell you about three thieves I know—each a true story. One of them is a fellow named Emanuel Ninger. The scene is in a little grocery store in a neighborhood in the year 1887. A man in his early sixties is in there buying some food; some turnip greens is one of the things he is purchasing. And he gives the clerk a $20 bill. The clerk's hands were little bit wet in the process of taking the wet turnip greens and wrapping them in a bag or some paper. As a result of her hands getting wet and holding the $20 bill, she happened to notice that some ink was coming off on her hand. She looked at the man who had given it to her and it was Emanuel Ninger, a neighbor, a friend, a customer for many years.

She was puzzled. Surely Emanuel Ninger would not give her a counterfeit $20 bill. Oh, no. No way. So she gave him his change. But in 1887, $20 represented a substantial sum of money, so she decided to tell the police. Two policemen came and looked at it. One said, "Ma'am, I'd like to have a thousand of them." The other one says, "Well, if it's so good, why is the ink coming off?"

Well, duty demanded that they get a search warrant. They did. They searched Mr. Ninger's home. They didn't find anything until they got to the attic, and there they found the paraphernalia for reproducing $20 bills. The things there were very simple—an artist easel, some brushes, some paint, and some paper. Emanuel Ninger was a very talented artist. Meticulously, stroke by stroke, he was painting those $20 bills.

While the police were up in the attic, they also found three portraits. The portraits at auction sold for a little over $16,000. The intriguing fact is that it took Emanuel Ninger almost exactly as long to paint a $20 bill as it did a portrait, which sold for well over $15,000.

Emanuel Ninger was a thief for sure, but the one from whom he was really stealing was Emanuel Ninger. As a talented artist, he could have made a substantial contribution to society while also enjoying a lifestyle that really would have been infinitely better. He was a thief. There's no question about it.

The second thief is a fellow named Arthur Barry. It's the roaring '20s and he was a jewel thief, and he was a good one. He worked in the Boston area. He became known as the "Gentleman Jewel Thief" because Arthur Barry only stole from the upper echelons of high society. As a matter of fact, it became somewhat of a mark of honor to have been called on and robbed by Arthur Barry. The society ladies discussed and asked the question, "Has Arthur Barry come calling on you yet?"

But the police took a little different view of Arthur Barry's activities. They laid a trap. They caught him in the act and shot him three times. With splinters of glass in his eyes and bullets in his body, he made a statement, which is not at all surprising. He said, "I'm not going to do this anymore."

Somehow or other, he managed to make his escape and for several years he lived outside the limits of the law as a free man. Then a jealous woman turned him in and he served many years in the federal prison. When he was released, he kept his promise. He did not go back to the life of being a jewel thief. He settled in a small New England town and became a model citizen. They elected him the commander of the local veterans' organization, and he served with distinction.

But as word will do, it leaked out. Reporters gathered around to interview the famous jewel thief of an earlier era. One of them asked the question, "Mr. Barry, you stole from an awful lot of wealthy people. But tell me, from whom did you steal the most?" Without a moment's hesitation Arthur Barry said, "The man from whom I stole the most was Arthur Barry. I could've been a baron on Wall Street. I could have been a very successful businessman. Instead, I spent two thirds of my life behind bars."

I believe humans are designed for accomplishment, engineered for success, and endowed with the seeds of greatness.

The third thief I would like to talk about is you. I believe that any man and any woman is a thief who does not recognize the inherent potential which is within them. I believe humans are designed for accomplishment. I believe we are engineered for success and endowed with the seeds of greatness. And I believe that the failure to recognize our own potential means that we're depriving ourselves and our families and society in general of what we as individuals could produce.

As I start discussing along these lines, I'm not going to be talking about developing a super-inflated, "I-am-the-greatest kind of an ego." Conceit is a weird disease. It makes everybody sick except the one who has it.

HEALTHY SELF-ACCEPTANCE

What I will be revealing is how to have a very healthy self-acceptance.

Most of your neighbors would never recognize you as a thief. They figure you're a good person. They recognize you as someone of character. They recognize you as a person of distinction. And yet I will say again and again—unless you begin to recognize your potential, you really are a thief.

What happens when we recognize ourselves for what we are and acknowledge the fact that we are unique and different, that we do have ability, that we do have talent?

One of my favorite true stories involves a fellow named Victor Serebriakoff. Now that's a tongue-twister of a name! When Victor was about sixteen years old, one of his teachers one day said to him, "Victor, you're a dunce. You're never going to be able to graduate from school. You're not going to be able to do anything with your life of any significance. Why don't you just drop out, learn a trade, get a job? At least you can be self-supporting."

Well, here's the voice of an authority saying, "You don't have it." And like too many people have done in the past, Victor in essence said, "Yes sir," or, "Yes ma'am," whatever the case might have been, and he dropped out of school. He became an itinerant for the next sixteen years. He did any number of odd jobs including a stint in the army. And then he was given some kind of IQ or evaluation test and they discovered that his IQ was 161!

We will perform in the same manner in which we see ourselves.

Let me emphasize that up until this point, Victor Sere-briakoff had been getting up every morning as a dunce, dressing a dunce, shaving a dunce, going to work as a dunce, and performing as a dunce. We will perform in the same manner in which we see ourselves. Victor was getting paid at the dunce's pay window.

And then one day without learning anything else, they didn't give him any additional information, they simply revealed what was already there. They said, "Victor, you've got an IQ of 161. You're a genius."

When Victor heard that, a change took place. He now started getting up in the morning and dressing as a genius, shaving a genius, going to work as a genius, and performing as a genius. He became a very, very successful businessman, a successful author. He became the international president of the Mensa Society—an IQ of 140 or higher is a requirement to join the Mensa Society. Remarkable change happened when Victor really saw himself for what he was.

Makes you wonder, for example, how many geniuses have never really recognized their own value.

Mildred Newman and Dr. Bernard Berkowitz wrote a book entitled *How to Be Your Own Best Friend.* They ask a rather penetrating question: "If we cannot love ourselves, where will we draw our love for anyone else?" The Bible says, "Love thy neighbor as thyself," presupposing that we in fact do love ourselves. Dr. Maxwell Maltz said that the goal of all psychotherapy is to change our self-image.

What role does our self-image play in our lives? A Gallup poll was conducted and it was reported on by Leroy Pope, a UPI business writer. He says that self-esteem should not be confused with egoism. A criminal or a megalomaniac has great egoism. Self-esteem from the sociologist's point of view is based on positive attitudes. The Gallup organization said the standard used in the poll is the Rosenberg Self-Esteem Scale developed by a widely known sociologist, Dr. Morris Rosenberg, and based on the answers of individuals to a series of questions about their attitudes toward themselves.

The study showed that 37 percent of Americans have high self-esteem —just 37 percent. The study also revealed that one of the most important findings was that persons with low self-esteem tend to suffer from a lot of physical and emotional stress and have high absentee rates on the job. That definitely diminishes productivity.

But the tests go beyond that. They show the elements usually conducive to high self-esteem are good family relationships, good moral standards, religion, close friends, financial well-being, hobbies, and status. We need to look there for what we can do to improve our self-image.

In the July 1986 issue of *Psychology Today*, psychologists Mary Ellen Fisher and Harold Lichtenberg questioned more than five hundred Vermont schoolchildren to gauge their long-term outlook in factors in their lives that may have affected it. They tested the fourth, fifth, and sixth graders in three sessions measuring their self-esteem, popularity with peers, and expectations for success as adults.

The elements usually conducive to high self-esteem are good family relationships, good moral standards, religion, close friends, financial well-being, hobbies, and status.

The children expressed strong anticipation of success and adulthood, and not much expectancy of failure. Fisher and Lichtenberg say that regardless of their age, sex, or personality, only their current level of self-esteem affected their outlook.

The way you see yourself today, in other words, affects your performance today. Now, the good news is simply this—regardless of how you see yourself now or in the past, you definitely, positively, and emphatically can change. If you don't like yourself, don't worry about it. You are not stuck with you as you are. And that is very good news.

VISUALIZATION

We need, however, to understand that the picture we have in our mind of ourselves has a major influence on our performance now and in the future. So the visualization process is something I'd like to consider for a moment; because whatever picture we painted our mind, the mind goes to work to complete.

For example, you've probably heard this scenario before. If we were to take a twelve-inch-wide plank and lay it on the floor and invite a friend to walk the plank, the friend would automatically think, *Why, that's an exercise in futility. That's an insult. My two-year-old child can do that.* But if we were to take the same twelve-inch-wide plank, stretch it between two twenty-story buildings, and then say, "Come walk the plank," the friend would undoubtedly say, "You've got to be out of your mind. I would fall and break my neck from a distance of twenty stories up in the air. I understand the plank is still the same width, but it's in a different position!" The picture our friend would have of the walk would be altogether different.

Jack Nicklaus, the great golfer—some say the greatest ever, having won more Masters championships than anyone else—says that the best practice he gets is when he is on an airplane on the way to the golf course before he ever gets there. That's his most important practice. He visualizes every single shot on that golf course and plays it in his mind. He sees those putts going in each cup. He always visualizes success before he ever strokes the ball.

If you don't see yourself as a winner, you cannot perform as a winner.

Motivation and positive thinking won't work for people who do not believe that they themselves are capable of doing anything they set their minds to. If they don't see themselves as winners, then they cannot perform as winners. Sometimes people with remarkable ability who should have good self-images don't think of themselves with a healthy attitude. It's not your age, your education, your physical appearance, your IQ, or anything like that that is important. We've got to acknowledge that all of those things are factors when we talk about our self-esteem.

I remember a number of years ago—before it became dangerous to pick up hitchhikers—I was in North Carolina, just outside of Raleigh, driving to Atlanta, Georgia.

I saw a hitchhiker with his thumb out and thought, *It's going to be a fairly long drive.* I looked forward to having a little company, so I stopped and the man got in the car. No sooner had he sat down when I became aware of the fact that maybe I had made a mistake. It was obvious that he had been drinking, and his opening comment was, "I just got out of prison today."

Well, that comment kind of has a tendency to tighten the conversation just a little bit, so I wanted to relax it as much as possible and said, "Well, I'm delighted to see that you're out. What were you in there for?"

He said, "Well, I was in there for moonshinin'."

And I said, "Well, how long were you there?"

He said, "Oh, a couple of years."

I said, "Well, did you learn anything while you were there?"

And he said, "What do you mean?"

I said, "Did you learn anything that will enable you to go back into society and be a more productive member of society?"

"Well," he said, "yes I did. I learned the name of every county in every state in America, and all of the parishes in Louisiana."

I said, "You've got to be kidding."

He said, "No, I know them all. Try me on one."

Well, I lived in South Carolina a number of years, so I said, "How about South Carolina."

He said, "Abbeville, Anderson..." And he went right down the list. He named every county. Then he said, "Think of another one."

I said, "No, you've convinced me."

Now there was a man who had an obviously limited education. And yet he had a very alert mind. I don't know what he would do with that information. The only possible use that I can think of is if he ever gets invited to appear on a quiz show and they ask, "Tell me the name of every county in every state in America," that old boy is probably the only one who could answer correctly.

What I'm getting at is this: had his self-image been compatible with his IQ, he undoubtedly would have learned some things that would have stood him in good stead.

Several years ago, I read that the janitor at the city hall in Portland, Oregon had an IQ of 173. I was intrigued with that and I was intrigued with the interview. Somebody asked him why on earth a man with an IQ of 173 was working as a janitor at city hall. And he said, "I wanted to get a job where nobody could take advantage of me."

Well, I don't know how you feel about dealing with a dude who has an IQ of 173, but if I were dealing with one, *I* would be the one worried about being taken advantage of. But I wouldn't be the least bit concerned about talking with a janitor. I'll guarantee you.

Now isn't that the weirdest thing you have ever heard? This guy didn't want anybody to take advantage of him. Well, as I understand the pecking order, the janitor is more likely to be taken advantage of than a lot of other people—but his self-image was such that he actually figured that was where he wanted to be.

Remember, education and intelligence are two different things. For example, Henry Ford left school at the age of fourteen, yet we know that he was a very intelligent man. The three of the most successful people I've ever met in my life only finished the third grade, the fifth grade, and the eighth grade. They were very successful and had very high IQs. Their education, formally, just happened to be a bit limited. I mention this because a lot of times people say, "Well, the reason I've got a low self-esteem is because I only finished…" and then they name whatever grade it might be.

LIFELONG LEARNING

Let me share with you something rather intriguing. At least it was to me. Did you know that if you have earned a Ph.D. then less than one half of 1 percent of the total knowledge you have acquired was learned in a formal educational setting? And that's if you have your Ph.D. The truth is, we rarely learn from other sources.

Did you know that by the time a child is six years old, two-thirds of everything they will ever know has already been learned? Did you know that by the time a child is three years old, according to a study done in Missouri, that two-thirds, 60 to 65 percent rather, of that child's working vocabulary has already been acquired by the age of three?

The learning process goes on all throughout our lives.

And why do I mention that? Simply to say that the learning process goes on all throughout our lives. And yet some people don't really achieve their success until they are aged forty or fifty or sixty or seventy or Grandma Moses. They don't really realize it until they get well on up in those years.

I don't care how many times the earth is going around the sun with you sitting on this ball of mud. That's not the important thing. The important thing is we need to understand that we can start today from where we are and make some changes that will make a very, very great difference.

Now, don't misunderstand. I'm not in any way putting down education. I fervently believe in it. Every year I average about two hours each day acquiring a better education. All I'm trying to say with that statement is your education is by no means confined to the classroom itself. If you're out of the classroom, that's one thing that you don't need to worry about. You can either go back to the classroom and learn more, or you can make your classroom life itself and learn what you need to know.

You *can* change your image.

CHAPTER 2

Start Early

You can change *what* you are and you can change *where* you are *by changing what goes into your mind.*

At the time of this writing, it is my absolute conviction that you can make $50,000 a year and be a failure, or you can make $10,000 a year and be a success. I'm talking about more than a standard of living, I'm talking about the quality of life. One person's ability might enable him or her to earn more than another. What we want to consider, though, is taking what we have and using it to the absolute optimum amount.

Success is not what you do compared to what somebody else does; it is what you do compared to what you are capable of doing with what you have and what you were given. What are the causes, basically, of some of our difficulties in life today? Our negative society is a major cause of a poor self-image.

Success is what you do compared to what you are capable of doing with what you have and what you were given.

Shad Helmstetter in his book *What to Say When You Talk to Your Self* writes that the average child, by the time they're eighteen years old, will have been told 148,000 times, "No," or, "You can't do it." Now when you're told that many times no or you can't do it, you will be inclined to believe it. We as individuals have been raised in a society that essentially is negative. Let me share with you just one or two incidents that I believe are indicative of what I'm talking about.

WORDS MATTER

How many times have you heard the phrase "Terrible twos"? I well remember this one particular day when I'd been out of town and returned home. Our first granddaughter was two years old at the time and as I walked in the front door, she looked up and said, "There's grandy!" She took off in a dead run straight for me—a magnificent specimen of femininity. Gorgeous long blond hair that any shampoo company in the world would be wise to seek an endorsement from. A smile that any toothpaste company ought to embrace just instantly, a personality that the kid stars on television would be envious of, and an intelligence that Einstein would have flipped over.

Now, I want you to understand that I say these things without bias, without prejudice, only as a grandfather would say. I'm just nailing in the fact. I took this gorgeous piece of femininity and threw her up and I caught her and held her in my arms. Then she looked right at me and said, "Love my grandy."

Can you imagine anybody saying "terrible twos"? They are the terrific twos, the tremendous threes, the fantastic fours, the fabulous fives, the super sixes, the sensational sevens. And guess where her self-image is because we believe that? That's right, she will have a healthy self image because that input has been enforced and reinforced.

So what is the basic problem?

We were having lunch in a cafeteria in Dallas one day and a little girl in front of us in line was crying. A grandmotherly type lady leaned down and said, "What's the matter, honey?" Her daddy spoke up and said, "She's mean, that's what. She's just plain mean."

I was in Atlanta, Georgia one time when a man brought his three little girls into my office. He introduced these beautiful little girls. "This is the one that won't eat. This is one that cries all the time. This is the one that won't mind their mother." What was he really doing? He was telling them right there—give me trouble, give me trouble, give me trouble. That's exactly what those little girls were hearing.

Many times I have complimented parents about their children saying, "What a well-spoken young man." Or, "My, what a smart young lady." Or, "What a good-natured child you have." Or, "He really is a gentleman." Or, "She is a wonderful child." Yet many parents then say, "Well, we've been very fortunate so far, but we know they're going to be teenagers one of these days." What are they doing when they say that? They are setting their kids up to rebel and give them trouble later on. It's astonishing.

I was in Nashville, Tennessee at the airport walking down toward the gate to catch a plane. I passed a mother and her little boy, a little guy about four or five years old, good looking little guy. And as I walked past, he was dragging his heels. You know, since Adam and Eve, no child has ever walked at exactly the right speed. And as I walked past, the mother turned to the child and said, "Come on, stupid, we're going to miss the plane!" Verbatim.

I was in Fresno, California jogging in the park. As I was running, I passed a grandmother and her granddaughter. A little girl about five years old, beautiful child. (Well, I'll tell you how pretty she was—she compares favorably with my granddaughter. If that doesn't tell you something about that child, I don't know what does.) As I ran past, the only words I heard were these, "They will put you in jail for that." Four or five years old, they're going to put her in jail? What a damaging comment.

Bill Glass, who had prison crusades all across the United States and is a former all-pro for the Cleveland Browns, says that more than 90 percent of the men and women in our prisons today were repeatedly told by their parents, "One of these days you're going to end up in jail."

Jim Sundberg, the great catcher who played for the Texas Rangers and later for the world champion Kansas City Royals, said that when he was a child in Fresno, California, his father consistently said to him, "One of these days, you're going to grow up and be a great Major League ballplayer." Jim was working with Bill Glass in a crusade in one of the prisons. During one of the breaks, just in casual conversation, Jim said to Bill, "You know, I'm so glad I didn't grow up and disappoint my dad." A prisoner standing close by overheard and said, "Well, you know what? I really didn't grow up and disappoint my dad. I'm exactly where he said I was going to be."

Had those two fathers in Dallas and Atlanta, the mother in Nashville, or the grandmother in Fresno come to me and said, "What would you suggest I do to destroy the self-image, the winning attitude, the enthusiasm, the zest for life, the creativity, the excitement, the loving and the caring…what would you suggest I do to destroy these things in my child?" I would have said to each of them, "Just keep it up, you're on the right track."

FAITH IN THE FUTURE—POWER IN THE PRESENT

All of that to say that one of the major causes of poor self-image is the fact that the input into the mind of the child is so negative in so many, too many cases. If you are from a background like that, don't hang your head on that window any longer. Your past does have an important bearing on your present, but as I will keep repeating what Dr. Tony Campolo says, "Your past is important as it relates to your present, but it is not as important as the way you see your future."

Your past is not as important as the way you see your future.

My friend John Maxwell puts it this way, "If there's faith in the future, there is power in the present." We will constantly be harping on developing that faith in the future by having you see who you are and what your capabilities are. Dr. J. Allen Peterson says that there are three things we can do for our children to give them a magnificent start in life. And these three things, with slight adaptations, apply wonderfully well for adults too. He calls them the three A's—*acceptance, affection,* and *approval.*

The first A is *acceptance.* Everybody wants to be accepted. If we accept our children unconditionally, then we give them the feeling of belonging, the feeling of assurance that will make a difference in their lives in a very positive way.

The second A is *affection.* It does make a difference. This is particularly true, Dad, for your little boys. Dr. Ross Campbell, psychiatrist from Chattanooga, says that the average six-year-old boy only receives one-sixth as much hugging and kissing as the average little six-year-old girl. He points out that in the first grade, little boys get in six times as much trouble as little girls. They are nine times as likely to have speech difficulties; and by the age of ten are ten times as likely to need psychological counseling as little girls. He goes on to say that in all of these years of research and practice, he's never known a single human being with a sexual dysfunction who had a father who was kind, considerate, thoughtful, and affectionate.

And yet there are a lot of "macho guys" who say, "If I kiss my little boy and make a sissy out of him," when the exact opposite is true affection. Now, the reason I harped on Dad is because I know most moms are going to give their little boy all of the hugging and kissing they need. Dad does a pretty good job until the little guy gets up to about four or five years old. And then when the child needs it the most, that's when they start holding it back from him. That's when the difficulties start. When these kids are eight or nine years old, they think that being hugged is the last thing in the world they want. But, let me tell you, that is the first thing they want. They're supposed to reject it because their buddies are rejecting it. But that's when it gets to be extraordinarily important.

The third A is *approval*. When we give them approval and they receive it from us, then there'll be no need to get involved with drugs or have a sexual relationship at an early age. They don't have to do those things because they have approval at home. Instead of the usual procedure that so many parents unfortunately follow, we want to be on the positive side. What do I mean by usual procedure?

Be on the positive side.

For example, the child brings home a test of twenty questions. He gets eighteen of them right. The two that are wrong are marked in red. And which ones do we put the emphasis on? The wrong two—not on all of the ones he got right.

We make overarching comments like, "Well, you *never* look nice." Yet there's a lot of difference between being sloppy one day versus never looking nice. "You're *always* dropping things," when a child drops a plate or dish or something of that nature. Be careful when using *always* or *never*, which can overdramatize situations. We need to be very careful about what we say. We need to deal with what the child or the employee *did*. Not the child or the employee. You criticize what happened, not berate the individual. You deal with the situation.

What are some other causes of a poor self-image? For one example, an individual can have a good self-image all of his or her life, but it can be destroyed with one traumatizing moment. When a husband or wife announces, "It's over. I've found somebody else," the damage that does to a person's self-image is inconceivable in the minds of people who have never experienced it. It is devastating.

A person could have been a valued employee, a breadwinner. Honest and true and faithful all of these years and then one day there's a merger or management changes and the individual loses his or her job. Sometimes an athlete, for example, can play a superb football game, and then fumble at the last instant. Everybody calls attention to the one thing that went wrong, instead of all of the things that went right—and it can have an impact on the person's self-image.

Sometimes in our society, according to Dr. James Dobson, too much importance is placed on brains and beauty. Everything goes along those lines—attention, promotions, favors, etc. And I've got to confess a little guilt; I personally have a tendency to lean that way. I've noticed in society that the very attractive child gets an incredible amount of attention; but the child who is not attractive to anyone except Mom and Dad does not get much attention. What society is really saying is unless you're physically attractive, or unless you're bright, you're really not going to get very far in this world of ours.

THE QUALITIES OF SUCCESS

The president of our company pointed out that we have eighty-plus employees. We did not hire any of them because they were handsome or beautiful. Now it just so happens that some of them are handsome and some of them are beautiful, but they were hired because, without exception, they have honesty and character and integrity, and they're loyal, they're trusting, they have great love, wonderful attitudes, good images, and good relationships.

Their goal is set—they understand that you can have everything in life you want if you just help enough other people get what they want. We believe those are the important things. Yes, some of them are extraordinarily bright also. We must obviously have that. But I share a lot of other people's sentiment. If a person is dishonest, I hope he's dumb. I'd hate to have a smart crook working for me, I really would; I'd much rather have a dumb one on the payroll.

So what do we look for first of all? Integrity. What causes a poor self-image? Sometimes a person can have a birthmark, and that will cause an undue amount of attention. They could be too tall or too short according to some people. They might be too fat or too thin, might have a weak chin, whatever on earth that is, they might have poor teeth. A lot of people, because of our emphasis on physical beauty, when they see an individual or when that individual looks in the mirror, they judge a multibillion-dollar personality and value based on the fact that they might not have every physical qualification that is necessary or that is "desirable" in our society.

I think of three people: I think of Eleanor Roosevelt; I think of Jimmy Durante; I think of Humphrey Bogart. As I look at these people, none of them were physically very attractive. Eleanor Roosevelt, the first time she stood up to make a speech, she passed out dead cold right then and there. I don't think she would have won a beauty contest on the best day she ever had. But she took what she did have, which was a very alert and sharp mind, a compassion for other people, a zeal for life, an interest in seeing things done right, and became one of the most respected people of her time.

I look at somebody like Jimmy Durante. Jimmy Durante was not exactly poster material. He had a nose which was roughly twice as big apparently as anybody else's. It could have been a big stumbling block for him. Instead, he constantly called people's attention to it and from that, he literally made his fortune. He took the lemon and created the lemonade that we all hear about it.

Humphrey Bogart would not have won a male beauty contest, either. But he took his ruggedness and applied his talent and became the envy of millions of people, millions of men who might have been more attractive physically, but he had that certain something—and he developed that certain something.

And I think of a thirty-eight-year-old woman who said she was born ugly, and then somebody scared her. In other words, she was not a beauty queen. At age thirty-eight, she picked up a self-improvement book, she read it, and she bought the idea that she could do something with her life. She remembered that when she was in college, she had the capacity to make a lot of people laugh. So she chose to make people laugh as a career. Phyllis Diller went on to earn as much as a million dollars in one year. Later, she had a lot of plastic surgery, and Phyllis Diller was far more attractive than she was thirty years previous when charting her future.

Those stories say really two things: 1) You take what you have and 2) you use it.

Take what you have and use it!

CHAPTER 3

No Comparisons, Please

Another cause of poor self-image is the use of unfair comparisons of experiences, which really have nothing to do with ability. For example, when we lived on Dilbeck Lane in Dallas, there'd been a lot of rain one night, and for some weird reason, which I'll never be able to understand, I decided that night of all nights I was going to put my car in the garage. I decided to drive down the back alley, which was not paved. That was mistake number one. I got stuck hopelessly just outside of my own house, there in the back alley. I worked and I sweated and I burned a little rubber and so forth trying to get out of the mud that night.

Finally I thought, *Well, nobody else is going to be foolish enough to try to come down this alley tonight. I'll just leave it here overnight.*

The next morning I called for a tow truck. Negative people call for wreckers, but at that point, I needed a tow truck to get out of there. The guy came and took a look at it. Incidentally, before I called him I had been out there trying to get the car out again. I'd thrown sand and bricks and boards and I'd burned enough rubber to drive from there to Jackson, Mississippi and back trying to get out of that hole.

Finally I gave up in frustration and called for a tow truck. This old guy looked at it for a minute and said, "Let me have your keys."

I said, "What're you going to do with them?"

He said, "I believe I can drive this car out."

I said, "Man, there ain't no way. I've been working on this thing last night and this morning."

He said, "Well, I'd like to give it a try."

Because I'm such a gracious kind, considerate, understanding fella, I didn't want to embarrass the old fella, and so I gave him my keys. I was all prepared when he failed to be kind and gracious about it. I was going to say, "Well, it was buried in there pretty deep, but don't feel badly about it. I mean, I worked at it myself trying to get out of here."

He got in the car, turned on the ignition, cranked the engine, turned the car just a tad to the left, rocked it twice, and in about seven seconds drove it right out of there, just slicker than a button. It was so easy that when he circled the block and came back, he was embarrassed about it. He wouldn't even look me in the eye.

I said, "Man, how on earth did you manage to do that?"

"Well," he said, "I was raised over here in east Texas and I've been driving out of gullies deeper than that since I was twelve years old."

Now that fella was not smarter than I was—he just had a different experience. See, don't ever feel inferior because somebody else has had a different experience. I would be absolutely lost back in our shipping department. I really would. Trying to ship something at the right price to the right place and have it labeled correctly, I would be lost.

Don't compare experiences.

A lot of times, for example, we look at doctors in absolute awe, and that includes me. I am amazed that they can even learn those big words, much less identify them with certain parts of the body and certain ways you feel and all that kind of good stuff, but when you realize the number of years they went to school, the thousands of hours they spent in preparation, the chances are good that if you had spent the same amount of time or I had spent the same amount of time, we too could be physicians.

I'll bet you nine dollars to a nickel, my favorite non-bet, if that brilliant physician were given your job right now, he would be totally incapable of handling it until he had acquired the experience that you have of handling it. It is fine to admire other people and other professionals. I do. I know you do, too. It's fine to admire them, but that's got nothing to do with your position on the totem pole. You are good at what you do and you can get better at what you do.

There are roughly a billion Chinese people on the face of this earth and all of them a year old and older can do something that I can't do and I'll bet you can't either. They can speak Chinese. Now does that mean they're smarter than we are or does it just mean that they've had a different experience? There are about seven million Australians who can do something that would scare me to death. They can drive down the wrong side of the highway. Now does that mean they're smarter than we are? No. It just means they've had a different experience.

What I'm saying out of all of this is you need to concentrate on the positive and not the negative. Don't feel inferior because somebody else can do something better than you can.

I was listing the things the other day that I cannot do. I cannot really fill out my own tax form. I couldn't take out my own tonsils. I can't repair my own teeth. I know nothing about repairing an automobile. As a matter of fact, I had a mechanical bypass when I was very young. I cannot fix anything of an electrical nature. There are thousands of things I cannot do. Now that doesn't bother me and I hope it doesn't bother you that other people can do those things. I know how to talk and I know how to write and those are the things on which I concentrate. What am I saying? I'm saying *find your strength and develop those strengths.*

Concentrate on the positive— not the negative.

Nine years ago I realized I was not a good businessman. Now that took some admission, but I realized that I was not, so I started looking for an individual who was organized, who knew how to run a business, who was a good manager, and that's where Ron entered the picture. At the time he came aboard, there were about a dozen of us; now there are over eighty. Hiring him freed me to do the things I can do. I brought somebody else in to do the things he can do well.

Since we cannot be champions at everything, many people have a natural tendency to play down the talents or qualities in which they *do* excel. In the process, we occasionally end up with phony humility. *We shouldn't think in terms of being better or worse than anyone else. As individuals, we are unique and different from anybody else.*

There have been approximately 11 billion people to walk this earth. There has never been two who were exactly alike. I can honestly say to you that you truly are unique. You very definitely are different. We need to understand that. It will help our self-image.

At one of the sessions, a lady came up to me and said, "Mr. Ziglar, I'm thirty-two years old. I have your tapes. On one of the tapes you keep saying, 'Tell your children that you love them. Tell them that you love them.'" She said, "In my thirty-two years of life, nobody has ever told me they loved me. I've never said to my little girls who are eight and ten years old that I love them, but I kept playing that tape and you kept telling me, 'Tell them you love them. Tell them you love them.' You even said that if you don't tell them, when they grow up and get married, they will never tell your grandchildren that they are loved. Somebody *has* to break the chain."

"One day," she said, "I blurted out that I loved them. They were in considerable shock for a moment and then they both grabbed me and started hugging…and from then on it was much easier."

"Mr. Ziglar," she said, "you cannot believe the psychological problems that my two little girls had. They were terrible, awful, including a reversion to infantile behavior—but within sixty days after I started telling them that I loved them, 98 percent of those psychological problems were solved."

The ancient prophet said it well when he said that love never fails. I'm just absolutely convinced that love will overcome an awful lot of mistakes.

Now, please understand. The last thing I ever want to do is hang a guilt trip on anybody. The past is behind us, and if we go back and say, "Oh, if I'd done this, things would have been different," then I have failed in my message to you. We want to look to the future. I'm convinced as a parent, though I made many mistakes, we did in my family the best we could with the information we had under the circumstances that existed at that time. I'm confident that you did, or are doing, exactly the same thing.

You can do something about the future—you can do nothing about the past.

Let's forget the past except using the experience as a learning experience. Let's take new information and a new look at the future, using what we have. We can *do* something about the future—there's nothing we can do about the past.

CHAPTER 4

Poor Self-Image Manifestations

We're going to now go to the second phase of self-image.

This old boy was walking down the street talking to himself and somebody stopped him and said, "Look here, partner, why do you talk to yourself?"

He said, "Well, it's two reasons. First of all, I like to talk to intelligent people. Second, I like to hear intelligent people talk."

Now I would say that he had a pretty good self-image. Incidentally, Dr. Joyce Brothers says that people who talk to themselves are slightly above average in intelligence. Those of you who've been doing that, I encourage you, just go ahead. I would also like to express a personal opinion. It is my opinion that it is all right to answer yourself, but if you ever catch yourself saying, "Huh?" then you know you've taken it too far. That's overdoing it. We don't want to get to that degree.

I was raised in the little town of Yazoo City, Mississippi, and I know that a lot of folks go around the country trying to impress people by claiming to be from Yazoo City, but I really am. I was born in LA, as in Lower Alabama, and raised there in Yazoo City. Not a big place; our Avon lady doubles as the church bell. It's small. Main Street runs through the car wash. We've hung a mirror up at the end of Main Street to make the town look bigger. We don't have a village drunk; a committee shares that responsibility. We had an urban renewal project underway and we wanted to paint a stripe down Main Street, had to widen the street first—not a big place.

I feel very comfortable in teasing about my hometown and let me tell you why I feel comfortable. Yazoo City is the home of the former president of the American Medical Association. It's home of the former president of the American Bar Association, home of the former president and vice president of the Southern Baptist Convention, and home of comedian Jerry Clower. It's the home of the former president and publisher of *Harper's* magazine, home of several distinguished jurists. I have no idea what happened to the other three. I can tease about the town folk because they have a good image because of what they have done in life.

Someone with a good self-image can take some kidding.

One of the ways you can tell whether a person has a good, healthy self-image is the way they can handle somebody kidding them a little bit. The person without a good, healthy self-image just simply cannot handle it when somebody is teasing them a little bit. They take it very personally. They regard it as a put down, not really realizing that the right kind of teasing really is a compliment to them.

CONFRONTATION

Confrontation does not always bring a solution to the problem; but until you confront the problem, there's going to be no solution to the problem. What we're going to do in this chapter is look at the manifestations of a poor self-image. If we recognize the manifestations in others and in ourselves, then we can confront that problem; we can deal with that problem. When we identify the problem itself, we've just taken a major step toward solving the problem.

As a young salesman, I had a very serious self-image problem. I was in direct sales for fourteen years. I cannot begin to tell you the number of times I would get out to knock on doors. That's what I did every day. I would call on one prospect and then instead of going next door, I would drive twenty miles down the highway to see another one. I told myself that I had to plan what I was going to say. I would rationalize that if I had the right approach, I would be able to get in the house and sell to them. I was rejected here, therefore I was not ready to go next door. I used the excuse that I was planning what I was going to say. The reality is I could not handle another rejection that quickly—which simply meant that I had a poor self-image.

Now I use the word "rejection" very deliberately because a lot of people use that word and think along those lines. Had I understood what Fred Smith talks about in his book *You and Your Network,* I would have been much more successful much earlier in my sales career.

Fred says that when people are rude and reject you, what they are really doing is not rejecting you personally. He says that is not a rejection, it is a business refusal. And they would have refused anyone who came knocking. It's not you, has nothing to do with you. He also says that when people are downright ugly to you, it is not in most cases because they want to hurt you; it is because they themselves are hurting. And if we can understand that, it enables us to deal with those people a lot more effectively and deal with ourselves a lot more effectively.

As a young salesman, on many occasions, I went out to go sell and instead I would go see prospects or customers whom I'd already sold. I had to service their equipment one more time. Now what I was doing was very simple. I was procrastinating. I'd go by the grocery store to get the baby a quart of milk although the refrigerator was overflowing with milk already. I'd hear a little click, click, click or a bump, bump, bump in that left front tire, so I'd go get it checked at the service station. I mean, really, I didn't want to get way out in the country and have tire trouble and couldn't get back to town. All of those are simply manifestations of a poor self-image.

My friend Chris Hegarty, who's one of the outstanding sales trainers in America, says that 63 percent of all sales interviews end with no attempt to close the sale. The salesperson talks and talks and talks, hoping that the prospect will finally say, "Okay, I'll take it." Then they will not have to lay their precious ego out on the line. The best way they can avoid being rejected is never to ask for the order. And some salespeople get very clever in doing exactly that. That's one reason you'll find a lot of salespeople in the movie theater in the afternoon. Now, you might wonder how I know they're in the theater in the afternoons. I saw them there; that's how I know they're there in the afternoons.

REJECTION OR REFUSAL

These excuses and diversions are simply manifestations of a poor self-image. We need to understand, therefore, what is the difference between refusal and rejection. Now my young son understands the two very clearly. When he would ask me for something as a child and I said no, he didn't feel the least bit rejected; he just felt like his dad had missed the question. He didn't get upset with me; he'd wait about five minutes and give me a chance to correct an obvious mistake. That's what we need to do—understand it's not a rejection when somebody turns down a request. Whether it is for a promotion, whether it's for a raise or whatever, it is a business decision in most cases that they are making. We need to handle it as such.

A lot of deserving people don't get raises or promotions because they don't know how to ask for them. They ask with the wrong attitude, with a chip on the shoulder, which is an indication of wood up above. They do not really approach it because they have felt rejected. They expect another turn-down, and in their minds it is a rejection. We need to understand if that is, indeed, our situation. A lot of people don't ask for raises because they, in their minds, don't see themselves getting a raise or promotion.

When we know we have earned a raise and are refused the raise, or if the employer says, "Yes, of course we're happy," or if they say "No," or "Maybe," don't get upset about it, simply say, "Well, I'm sure you have a logical reason from a business perspective as to why you're saying no at this time. Would you share with me what your reason is, number one? And number two, what can I do to earn the right to this raise or promotion? What can I do to make your job easier, this company more productive and more profitable?"

Look at both perspectives.

Now I guarantee you when you take the response in that light, your chances are going to be dramatically enhanced. The way you see you is very, very, very important. Also, the way you see your value to the company might be dramatically different from the way the boss sees it. We need to look at both perspectives.

My friend Bill Gove, who has been a professional speaker for many, many years, tells a story about this fella who was on trial for his life. He had been accused and charged with killing somebody and stuffing the person in a suitcase and trying to ship it across the border into Mexico. He was caught in the process and his lawyer was pleading his case. He said, "I know, ladies and gentlemen of the jury, what some of you might think. I know what the law thinks. They think of my client as a cold-blooded, heartless, murderous killer." He said, "The truth is, he was only caught because the thumb of the victim was sticking out of the suitcase. You see him as a murder, I see him as a lousy packer." Perspective can be quite different.

OBVIOUS MANIFESTATIONS

Let's take a look at some obvious manifestations of poor self-image.

Why do we need to know what the manifestations are of a poor self-image? When we recognize them, we can deal with them. I'll probably say that at least three times before you're through reading this book.

CAN'T ACCEPT COMPLIMENTS

A person with a poor self-image cannot accept a compliment.

For example, you say to that individual, "Oh, I just love that dress." And the response it, "This old thing?"

"My that's a beautiful suit you're wearing."

"Oh, I got it in a basement sale."

"This chicken is really delicious."

"Well, it should have been marinated a little bit longer."

"My that was an excellent report you turned in."

"Well, I wish I had had a little longer to get it ready…if they'd just told me earlier."

Some people just cannot accept a sincere compliment.

A simple thank you is all that is necessary after receiving a compliment. It would make everyone feel a lot better.

Poor self-image manifests itself in the way we handle our personal lives. When you tell a youngster with a poor self-image that he ought to stay away from drugs, they'll kill you. His response, at least internally, many times is, *Don't tell me that. My friends tell me that they make you feel good. Make you feel big. Besides, suppose they're not good for me, what difference does it make? I'm a nothing, I'm a nobody. Got nothing to lose.* A person with a good self-image would not respond in any such manner.

When you tell youngsters to study their lessons and obey the law, if they have a poor self-image, many times they're so negative they say, "It won't do me any good. The deck's already stacked. I came from the wrong side of the tracks. The rich kids are going to get all of their breaks, why shouldn't I have a little fun right now?"

When you say to a youngster with a poor self-image, "You really ought to save yourself for marriage." Their instant thinking is, *Who's going to marry me? What chance have I got? Why don't I have a little fun now? That's what it's all about. My peer group tells me I've got to do these things to be accepted. Since I have nothing to lose, why not go ahead?*

59

JEALOUS WITHOUT CAUSE

An individual with a poor self-image is jealous without cause. Now I'm not talking about jealousy for a cause. Lady, if he comes in smelling like joy and lipstick all over his collar, jealousy is not a manifestation of a poor self-image; that has nothing to do with it. But some people say, "Oh, I just love him so much, I can't let him out of my sight." Or, "I just love her so much, I don't want her out of my sight." What they're really saying is, "I don't understand why this person married me in the first place. I certainly do not deserve him or her."

A jealous, critical nature is one of the manifestations of a poor self-image. They can't handle constructive criticism, much less criticism itself. One of the interesting manifestations of a poor self-image is old "motor-mouth." We once had one who worked for us. Now there's a guy that if you asked him what time it was, he would tell you how to build a clock. I mean, literally, you have seen people who are like that. They corner you or they come visiting you and they start talking and they talk and they talk—incessantly they talk.

Finally you persuade them that it's time for them to leave or else they give you some indications that they're going to leave and they get to the front door and they open the door and they talk another five minutes there in the doorway. And if you happen to visit their house, and you're trying to leave, they follow you all the way out to the car; and as you're backing out, they're signaling you to roll down the window, they've got one more thing they want to tell you. I think you probably know exactly the type of person I'm talking about.

TOO NOISY OR TOO QUIET

The class clown is the typical example of an individual with a poor self-image. They come in a couple of minutes late, you know, and distract everything. "Oh, you already started class, Ms. Brown? Oh, did we have an assignment today?" They're people who feel they cannot attract any attention on their own. Therefore, they have to make a show.

Now on the other end of the scale, on occasion, quiet people also have a poor self-image. They think they have nothing at all to offer. They read somewhere that still water runs deep and that it is better to remain silent and let people think you're smart than to speak up and let everybody know you're not smart.

But let me stress that in the case of the class cut-up, the motor-mouth, or the quiet people, the key is that these personality traits could be manifestations of a poor self-image—but not always. If a person exhibits any of these three characteristics, he or she does not necessarily have a poor self-image, but the odds are pretty good that they do.

I mention this because if any of these characteristics describe you, the identification process will encourage you to take the necessary steps to do something about it. If they describe any of your friends, associates, or relatives, it will enable you to recognize them and to be of assistance to them.

LACK OF COMMITMENT

Another manifestation of a poor self-image is a lack of commitment. These people don't set goals. They figure, "If I make a commitment, if I set a goal, if I say that I'm going to do this, and then it doesn't work out, then it further destroys my self-image. Therefore, if I don't make the commitment, there's no way I can fail." Negative people seldom are very persistent because they simply do not believe they can accomplish any objectives.

MISTREAT OTHERS

Poor self-image is manifested, a lot of times, particularly in the way we treat people in a subservient position. One other thing that bothers me the most is when I see someone abuse another individual who cannot defend themselves. For example, a waiter or a waitress, in many cases, cannot properly defend themselves. A shipping clerk, file clerk, or somebody in an entry-level position usually cannot properly defend themselves.

The most irritated I've ever been with anybody is one day years ago when an associate of mine verbally abused my secretary. It was most unfair and completely uncalled for. If he wanted to fight, he should have fought with me. I can fight back. But she was not in a position to fight back. A person who will do that, you can put your last penny on it, there's an individual who really has a distorted sense of values and who also has a poor self-image.

TOO GENEROUS

A lot of times, new employees with a poor self-image will come in and make some unrealistic promises about what they can do. The new coach, teacher, or salesperson sometimes does exactly the same thing. A lot of kids with poor self-images insist on picking up the tab for the Cokes. When buddies get together, they think they don't deserve to be friends with anybody on their own merit, so they figure, *If I pick up the tab for the Cokes then they'll think I'm a good guy and they'll accept me as part of the group and I'll be invited back.*

Years and years ago when I was in sales management, I would watch salespeople who I knew were broke. So broke that if it cost fifty cents to go around the world, they couldn't even get out of sight. And yet I saw some of them absolutely insist on picking up the tab every time the group went out anywhere. They thought they could not be accepted on their own.

CLEANLINESS

Sometimes poor self-image is manifested in our penchant for cleanliness. For example, some household executives clean up immediately if a tiny drop of coffee spills when you set the cup back down in the saucer. They clean up the ashtrays before someone finishes smoking the first cigarette. I heard about this one lady who was so fastidious that when her husband got up to go to the bathroom during the night, she had the bed made when he got back. That's kind of overdoing it, I believe, and it does indicate something.

AFRAID TO DISCIPLINE

Another manifestation of a poor self-image are the parents who never discipline their children. They fear that the child will withhold love from them—and they just love them so much, they say, that they cannot do any disciplining. What that really means is that the parents don't completely love the child. They have such a fear that they will lose that love that they will do just about anything to keep that from happening. The tragedy is that in that process, they damage the relationship, they damage the child, and they damage that child's future. Parents who truly have a good self-image understand that real love demands that they do for the child what is best for the child.

AFRAID TO QUESTION

A student who will not properly question the teacher about a grade or report could have a poor self-image. Now, there are certain ways to do it. You don't go up and stomp your foot and demand, "How come I got this C? I deserve a B." But rather, go up very quietly and say, "I was certainly disappointed in my grade. I wonder if you would explain to me what I need to do to bring it up, because I honestly thought it would be higher this time. Would you mind going over with me why the grade is not a B instead of a C?" I've never seen a responsible teacher who would not respond positively to it.

This also applies, as stated previously, for adults who are told no when asking for a raise or a promotion.

PROMISCUITY

The manifestation with the greatest long-range impact on our children, as far as self-image is concerned, occurs in the pre-teen or very early teenage years. When the child who has a poor self-image and does not have a lot of friends one day realizes that Johnny and Mary are different, that boys and girls are different. Johnny meets Mary and Johnny has been rejected in his mind all of his life, Mary's been rejected all of her life in her eyes, and now they discover each other. And they discover that chemistry is in more places than the laboratory. They kind of latch on to each other. For the first time, they find somebody who loves them just for themselves. And a very volatile situation gets underway.

That's one of the reasons the study done by Concerned Women for America shows something rather intriguing. Here's what they discovered: girls who start dating at age twelve, the odds are five to one that by the time they graduate from high school, they will be in a sexual relationship. Girls who start dating at age sixteen, the odds are five to one that they will not be involved in a sexual relationship by the time they finish high school. Very significant. The parents' self-image, therefore, plays a major role in the way they deal with their child. Many times a child comes home with incredible pressure to start dating. After all, all of her classmates are going out.

Parents' self-image affects the way they deal with their child.

I so well remember when our oldest daughter started putting the pressure on us. With tear-stained eyes, she said, "But Daddy, all of the good boys will be gone." I mean, she was just as serious about that as she could possibly be. I am so delighted that we were able to persuade her that all the good boys would not be gone by the time she got to be sixteen years old.

I remember another occasion when she wanted to go to such-and-such a place with such-and-such a group, and I said, "Of course you can't go."

And she said, "Why?" And she started to cloud up, you know.

I said, "Well, there are two basic reasons for it. It's the wrong group at the wrong place."

She used the standard response on me that every parent with teenagers has heard about 4,000 times. "But Daddy, everybody else is going."

I kind of smiled and said, "Now sweetheart, come on. You know perfectly good and well that's no reason for you to go."

She said, "Well, why can't I go?"

And I said, "Well, it's the wrong place and the wrong crowd. And I want to tell you something. These friends of yours right now, they might not even be speaking to you a year from today. And five years from today, you might not even remember their names. But I'm your daddy, and regardless of what you do, a year from now or ten years from now or fifty years from now, I'm still going to love you as much as I do today. And today I love you too much to let you put your reputation on the line by going to a place that is not in your best interest."

She paused there for just a moment and then she almost literally jumped forward, hugged me, and kissed me and said, "Thank you, Daddy. I didn't want to go anyhow."

Isn't that fascinating? I don't know what she told her buddies when she went back out there but she might have said to them, "Well, my daddy won't let me go anywhere. He won't let me do anything." That doesn't make any difference. I believe that she was ahead of the game because of it, and I believe that we were ahead of the game because we would not let her do that.

ILL-FITTING MASKS

Self-image is so important. The person with a poor self-image doesn't move successfully into management. He feels rejection by the people over him, under him or around him. He often steps out of character and dons one of four ill-fitting masks.

- First, he tries to be good-old Joe and assures his subordinates that nothing has changed. He desperately tries to be one of the gang.

- Second, in his fear of rejection by his former peers, he makes concessions and exceptions that go beyond the principles of good management. Sometimes he does the opposite and takes an arrogant, "I have arrived" approach, which causes resentment among his former peers.

- Third, he may be unduly concerned about his relationship with management and in his anxiety to please, he becomes too servile, eats too much humble pie, and seeks too much advice. He has an exaggerated fear of failure because he sees his worth in terms of never failing. Ironically, this fear of failure causes him to hesitate too long before taking any action. This unrealistic hesitancy is often the cause of failure.

- Fourth, the manager with a poor self-image may assume a know-it-all attitude, seek advice from no one, and set out to show everyone that he knows how to run the ship. A poor self-image is manifested in every walk of life; even good-old Joe or Josie have the problem, which is a common one and is no respecter of age, sex, education, size, or skin color. He has the, "I must be a nice guy and never offend anyone" kind of a self-image syndrome. And listen, as a youngster, he smokes cigarettes he doesn't want, takes a drink he doesn't like, laughs at dirty jokes that actually offend him, joins the gang he secretly dislikes and goes along with illegal or immoral conduct and participates in a dress code he secretly abhors—all because he has never accepted himself and is terribly concerned that if he asserts himself and crosses his peer group, he will not have any friends.

As an adult he has a tendency to tell people only what he thinks they want to hear. He would never send an over-cooked steak back to the kitchen. He even gives up his place in the barbershop, lets others take his parking spot or even crash the line in front of him. He doesn't argue with the boss, nor object when a coworker takes credit for work he has done. Now, don't misunderstand, if you are Joe and your self-image is so healthy, you can conduct yourself in this manner because this is what you want, that's okay.

If you view these incidents as minor or small stuff that mean nothing in your game plan for life, then your self-image is in excellent shape. However, if you do these things to gain acceptance, you're gaining everything *except* acceptance. The reason is simple—you are not presenting the real you; in fact, you are presenting a phony and most people, including other phonies, don't like a phony. The good news is this—there's something you can do about it.

In the next chapters, we're going to look at twenty-four specific steps you can take that will dramatically change your self-image for the better.

CHAPTER 5

Steps to a Healthy Self-Image

A lady named Jan McBarron lives in Columbus, Georgia. In 1977 she picked up my book titled *See You at the Top*. The first statement she read had an impact on her life: "You are the only person on the face of this earth who can use your ability; it is an awesome responsibility." She wrote me a letter about the book and told me, "I took that statement and started building on it, and that's when my life started to change."

As we look at the steps toward building a healthy self-image, the first thing I'm going to say is the one that really caught Jan's attention and really caused her to take action to make changes in her mindset: "Nobody on the face of this earth can make you feel inferior without your permission."

TWENTY-FOUR STEPS TO A HEALTHY SELF-IMAGE

Step One in building a good healthy self-image is to *absolutely refuse to give permission* to anyone who wants to make you feel inferior. Don't let anyone put you down.

Step Two: If you want to build a healthy self-image, you need to take an inventory of what you have. Every businessperson, if they expect to stay in business and in favor with "Uncle Sam," has to take inventory regularly. You need to take inventory because your assets are absolutely awesome. That's the only way I can describe them.

A number of years ago in Gary, Indiana, a lady went to the doctor because she had a rash on her face. He examined her, gave her a prescription for some drugs. She took the drugs. They settled in her eyes. She lost 98 percent of her sight. The insurance company paid her $1 million. Question: Would you swap places with her? She takes your eyes. You take her million dollars. There's no way you would do that, is there?

A lady in California was injured in an airplane accident. She broke her back. She will be flat on her back, they say, the rest of her life. The insurance company gave her a million dollars. The question is, would you swap places with her? And again I'm certain the answer would be a resounding no.

Do you know who Betty Grable was? If you do, you probably know she was a famous dancer and actress, best known for her shapely legs. Actually, she had arms and a head and the whole works you know, yet every time Betty Grable's name is mentioned, her legs are too. Now, why is that? Because her legs were insured for $1 million. I assume by that that her legs were worth a million dollars.

Now, at this precise moment, would you like to see another pair of million-dollar legs? If you just back up and take a good look at your very own, you will see a pair of million-dollar legs, if they will get you around at all. There's no way you would part with them for a million dollars would you?

Do you see what we've already done? We've looked at your eyes. They're worth a million. Your back's worth a million. Your legs are worth a million, and we haven't even considered the rest of you. It's awesome when we start examining what we are worth.

A few months ago a Rembrandt painting sold for in the neighborhood of $50 million. Now, that's some kind of neighborhood, isn't it? Fifty million dollars. And if you think about it, all in the world that is, is just some paint on a canvas put there in a very special way. Certainly, the paint is not worth that much. Certainly, the canvas is not worth that much, but it's the arrangement the artist made on the canvas that brought that price. Rembrandt was a genius, there's no question of that, and the painting was worth the money because of his creative genius and because it is the only one in the whole world. Its rarity gave it value.

Recognize and take an inventory of your talent and ability; you'll realize that you have enormous value.

Well, friend, you are far rarer. There have been eleven billion people to walk this earth, but there's never been one like you. You truly are rare. We'll never know how many Rembrandts we have walking loose. I mean people having the talent as Rembrandt, who've never taken the brush to the canvas and started to do the painting. How much talent do we have that is never really used? We will never know. But the purpose of this book is to get you to recognize your own ability and talent, and when you begin to take that physical inventory and an inventory of your talent, you'll realize that you do have enormous value—you're a natural champion.

Science confirms what I'm talking about. They estimate that if they could recreate the human brain, or even approximately, that it would require a building larger than the Empire State Building, that it would cost well over one hundred million dollars, that it would take more electricity to run it than is required to run a small city. And yet this man-made, hundred-million-dollar brain could not even begin to compete or compare with what you have between your ears.

Humans are absolutely remarkable—truly amazing. One simple example is that it takes seventy-two muscles to utter a single word. All those muscles perfectly coordinated to utter a word. We are truly remarkable. Self-image is important, and when you start taking that inventory, you realize that yes, indeed, you are definitely somebody special.

I would like you to consider the fact that the Bible verifies you are unique and somebody special. Ethel Waters was an American jazz singer and actress. I love what she had to say at a Billy Graham crusade in London, England. The crowds were enormous. Someone approached Ethel and asked, "How do you account for the amazing popularity of Mr. Graham?" Ethel Waters, as only Ethel Waters could, gave the man a big grin and said, "Honey, see God don't sponsor no flops. God doesn't sponsor flops. God doesn't make junk."

I love what my close friend Mary Crowley said before her death. She was a beautiful person and one of the most successful businesspeople I've ever encountered—wise beyond belief. Mary Crowley, with a twinkle in her eye and grin on her face, said, "God made man, took one look, and said I can do better than that, and made woman." I would not argue with that particular statement.

When we start talking along those lines, let's consider this scenario. Let's assume that your child came up to you and said, "I'm a nothing, I'm a nobody. Nobody likes me. I can't do anything. I'm just worthless."

If that should happen, it would really thrill you to death. You'd get all excited and you'd say, "That's right, honey, and I'm glad you've finally recognized that you're a loser. You're a nothing. You're a nobody." I know that's exactly the way you'd feel isn't it?

Or would it break your heart?

I wonder how God feels when we say, "Lord, let's face it. You blew it. You made a mistake. I mean I'm a loser all the way down."

I won't do it, but I can give you any number of Bible verses that say you're on dangerous ground when you criticize yourself. You're really criticizing your Maker when you criticize what He did with you.

Step Three: *If you want to build a good self-image, you need to* **make up and dress up and go up**. When my wife would go to the beauty shop, she'd come home walking proud. I mean, I never can understand what rearranging a few strands of hair does to women, but I guarantee you, it changes them significantly. It has a dramatic impact on self-image.

The interesting thing is, when you make up and dress up, you will go up, because your performance definitely is tied to the image you have of yourself. Male or female, if you're feeling attractive, if you're feeling well-dressed— you're feeling more confident. It just goes with the territory.

I've talked with any number of educators who tell me that on picture-taking day the conduct of the students is infinitely better than it is on a regular day. The kids show up well-dressed. They put on their best behavior, and their performance that day is better.

The way you dress does make an absolute difference in your attitude and self-confidence.

Years ago in some places across the country, they used to have what they call Sadie Hawkins Day. This is when the kids would go to school all dressed in old worn-out clothes. The day was discontinued because the conduct of the kids that day was absolutely abominable. They were destructive and rowdy and they got out of hand.

The way you dress does make an absolute difference in your attitude and self-confidence. You can't climb the ladder of success dressed in the costume of failure. The way you dress does make a difference. Now I'm not talking necessarily about investing a whole lot of money. I am talking about being clean and neat and doing the best you can with what you have. Step number three—if you want to build a healthy self-image, you need to get dressed up and take care of your appearance.

One of the things that's always been a mystery to me is men and women, husbands and wives, will dress up every day to put their best foot forward and look their best on their job and for their associates, and then on weekends they kind of let themselves go and look scroungy. They do not dress up and clean up for their mates, the most important person in their lives. Maybe that's one of the reasons that the American family experiences some of the trouble that they do.

Step Four: If you really want to build a healthy self-image, you need to read Horatio Alger stories. You need to read about Mary Crowley and what she did. You need to read about Ross Perot and what he's done. You need to read about Mary Kay Ash, about Roger Staubach, about Eartha White.

Eartha White's story is one of my favorites. It appeared in *Reader's Digest* back in December, I believe it was 1974.

That's a long time ago. Eartha was the daughter of an ex-slave. She was raised in Jacksonville, Florida, in a time when our country, particularly in the southern part of our country, had real serious prejudice problems. They still have some, but in those days in the South, it was almost total.

Nevertheless, Eartha made millions and millions of dollars under those circumstances and gave every dime to the furtherance of the causes in which she believed— essentially, in her people. You cannot read that story and not be moved. When you read it, you will say, "If she can do it, I can do it." It really will do wonders for you.

Read and identify with successful people.

Read the story of Mamie McCullough, our "I Can" lady, who had so many difficulties as a child. You will read about how she was abused and how she came from a home that was in pretty poor financial circumstances, difficulties that are unbelievable, and yet she came out the winner and stronger as a result of it all. When you read that story, you'll say, "If she can do it, so can I." Read and identify with successful people.

Step Five: Listen to speakers and teachers and preachers who build up and encourage people. Listen to or read books written by Paul Harvey or Bobbie Gee, who was one of the outstanding ladies I have ever met. I shared the platform with her about a dozen times a year. She was over 6 feet tall when she was thirteen years old. You can well imagine what that did to her as far as getting along with her classmates is concerned. She has a tremendous sense of humor and laughs about the fact that she would go to the dances, and the boys she was dancing with would have their nose in her navel. I mean she really is tall, but when you talk to her and listen to what she has to say, you'll realize that she's a lady who has her self-image in the place where it ought to be.

I encourage you to read books by Norman Vincent Peale, W.A. Criswell, Denis Waitley, Mamie McCullough, and Robert Schuller. Listen to the people who really build up the best in people.

Step Six: Take some short, easy steps. A lot of people fail because they try to take too big of a step too quickly. When the high jumper goes out to jump, if he can jump six feet, he doesn't go out and initially set the bar at six feet. He sets it at maybe four feet and takes a couple of easy jumps, then he moves it up and then moves it up and moves it up again.

Likewise, you don't move from two times two into analytical geometry or calculus. You don't go from oatmeal cookies to Baked Alaska. There are some steps in between that you need to take, which definitely does improve your confidence and increase your confidence.

When I was in the cookware business in direct sales, from time to time salespeople would hit a slump. Our set of cookware was relatively expensive. We had a little salad machine that went along with it, and in those days it sold for $19.95. When one of our people would hit a slump, I would take their cookware samples away from them, give them that salad machine only, and require that they go out and sell it.

Now, they knew they might not make a $150 sale, but because the $20 sale was so easy, they'd go out with considerable confidence. "Yeah, I know I can sell this!" Well, anybody can sell a $20 item, so when they came back with several of those sales, their confidence and optimism was up. Then we'd give them their samples back, and they would go out and sell the set of cookware. Take the easy step sometimes. When your image changes, you can perform better.

In Calhoun High School in Port Lavaca, the high jumper, after taking the "I Can" course, jumped 4 inches higher than he'd ever jumped before. He could literally see himself now as being a champion. Their pole vaulter set the national high school record, and he said it was a direct result of an improvement in his self-image.

*Step Seven: To build your self-image, you need to **join the smile, firm handshake, and compliment club**.* It's amazing what a smile will do for you and other people. It's a little curve that sets a lot of things straight, and if you see somebody who does not have a smile, they're bankrupt— so give them yours. A smile really does do an awful lot of things for someone else.

A good, firm handshake is essential to the development of a good, firm personality.

And the way you shake hands is so important. Some people give you a dead fish shake, and that makes you feel bad. Others just stick their hand out, and you grab it and it's like a windmill—you kind of pump it up and down. And there are others who get into a test of strength with you. A good, firm handshake is essential to the development of a good, firm personality.

What I'm really talking about here is the development of personality. Personality is the complete list of all of the characteristics you have. It's all of the qualities you have.

That's what really makes up personality. When you're accepted by others, that improves your image.

Start the youngsters early. Every time I meet a youngster, I shake hands with them, and if they do not give me the right handshake, I will say to them, "No, son, give me a little more, squeeze it a little harder." Then I say to them, "One day you're going to be looking for a job, and the way you shake hands with your prospective employer will play a role in whether you get that job or not."

Smile at people—young and old—look right into their eyes, give them that firm handshake, and when they accept you, that helps you accept you too! It improves your image.

Step Eight: *To build a healthy self-image,* **finish the job.** Finish the job! One of the signs of a poor self-image is the individual who doesn't quite finish reading the book or completing the report, or cutting the grass, or painting the fence, or cleaning the room. They never quite finish it. Now, if *you* finish doing those things, let me tell you what happens—people say nice things about you. They compliment you. That makes you feel good. Completion means compliments. It also means praise and it may mean a raise and promotion.

Completion means compliments.

I was one of those fortunate individuals who was raised by an outstanding lady who had incredible faith, was an enormously hard worker, and who taught us with a lot of sonnet-sermons. One of her favorites was this one; I bet I heard it seventeen thousand times; I will remember it forever and ever and ever. If you were to wake me up at 3 o'clock in the morning and say, "Zig, what did your momma say?" I could give it to you verbatim: *"When a task is once begun, you leave it not until it's done, and be a matter great or small, you do it well or not at all."*

I believe that if we will convey that message to our children, it will give them the sense of responsibility of completing it. It will help them gain acceptance, and it definitely will improve their self-image and the image others have of them.

Step Nine: *Do something for someone else.* David Dunn wrote a beautiful little book entitled *Try Giving Yourself Away.* As I was going through this reading, a friend wrote to me and said when she really understood the concept to "do something for somebody else who can do nothing in return for you, there's nothing else that will give you the satisfaction that does."

Visiting a shut-in, reading a book for the blind in a cassette recording. Being of service can really be helpful to people. Go see somebody at the hospital. Take someone a cake. Just go listen to a senior citizen.

Jan McBarron, mentioned at the beginning of this chapter, chose to teach the functionally illiterate how to read. She takes one adult at a time and she teaches that adult how to read, and when she goes through that process, she says, "It is the most exciting, the most rewarding thing you can possibly imagine. To see the expressions of hope light up and the expressions of delight that they now know what the newspaper says, that they can in fact understand things that they never could understand before, it makes you feel good." Helping others does lots of good for your self-image.

Helping others does lots of good for your self-image.

Charles Dickens said something that even the individual whose self-image is right on the bottom will have to relate to. He said, "No one is useless in this world who lightens the burden of it to anyone else."

Step Ten: *Be a quitter.* Quit smoking. Quit drinking. Quit swearing. Quit losing your temper. Quit eating too much. When you take charge and break a destructive habit, it does some wonderful, wonderful things for your image. When I lost thirty-seven pounds, taking control of that phase of my life, it made a dramatic difference in my own self-image.

In December of 1987, I hurt my back. Wasn't serious. All the doctor said was, "You can't jog and do those other things for a couple of months." In the next two months, I gained eight pounds. See, my body retains ice cream. Two months passed, and I started jogging again last week, and I've taken five of those pounds back off. I'll go ahead and get the rest of them off.

It absolutely makes a difference when you get rid of destructive habits.

I can tell you with absolute certainty, it does absolutely make a difference when you get rid of destructive habits. It gives you a feeling of power, a feeling of accomplishment. If you've had a violent temper and you can bring it under control, you will feel better about yourself. If you've had some destructive habit and you bring it under control, it really does a lot for your self-image. Quit doing those things that are destructive.

Step Eleven: Get even with your enemies. As a matter of fact, better than that, *get ahead of your enemies.* How do you do that? One of the reasons I love my Bible is because it is so practical. I do not understand how anybody can claim to be educated and have refused to read the all-time best seller.

Now, for those of you who don't understand the language of the King James Version, there are many other versions of the Bible available now that are written for every level of reader. The language is so clear and so simple, there is no mistaking the truth and wisdom.

Let me give you the reason when I talk about the Bible being practical. When Christ was walking the earth, He brought an unusual command to the people there. He said to them, "And if anyone wants to sue you and take your shirt, hand over your coat as well. If anyone forces you to go one mile, go with them two miles" (Matthew 5:40-41 New International Version).

Now, let me set the stage for you. Israel was under the dominion of Rome. Under Roman law, the citizens of Israel had to house for one year the Roman soldiers. If the Roman soldier said, "Take this armor one mile," they were required by law to take it one mile. When the soldier says, "Take it a mile," when you get through at the end of the mile, instead of slamming it down like they had been doing all of this time, Jesus says take it another mile. And do not just take it; when you are taking it, talk to the soldiers. Find out where they're from. Get acquainted with them. Ask about their family. When the Roman soldiers saw that attitude, an amazing thing happened. When Christianity was spread throughout the Roman empire, it was spread by the Roman soldiers.

Friend, you can have everything in life you want if you help enough other people get what they want. Deal with your enemies. Get ahead of them. Don't just get even with them. Make friends out of them. Go the extra mile.

CHAPTER 6

A Healthy Self-Image Lifestyle

Continuing with the twenty-four steps to a healthy self-image, I encourage you to make these steps part of your everyday lifestyle.

Step Twelve. Choose your friends and your associates carefully. I've been deeply concerned about the drug war for many years. One thing we've observed is that we can measure and predict with unerring accuracy who's going to get involved in drugs. Kids get involved in drugs in direct proportion to the number of times they are given the opportunity to get involved in drugs. If they are running with kids who are into drugs, the odds go up day by day by day that they're going to get into an experimental stage. We're influenced by the people around us. If they're good people, then we're influenced positively. If they're bad, we're influenced negatively.

To emphasize that fact, in Belleville, Illinois, at the Belleville Township High School West, there was an award called the High News Citizenship Award. There were eleven winners each year. Out of the eleven winners, a couple of years ago, four of them came out of one group of eleven people. These eleven kids, since they'd been in junior high school, with one exception, had the same classes, they went to school together, they spent weekends together, they were inseparable all of those years. All eleven of these kids made the finals and four of the nine in that school who received the award were in the same group. Your associates *do* make a difference.

Step Thirteen. *To build a good, healthy self-image,* **make a list of your positive qualities.** It's an absolute fact you can be just as honest, just as enthusiastic, just as conscientious, just as responsible, just as dependable, just as hardworking, just as friendly, just as...and go right down the list, as anybody on the face of this earth.

This sounds like the Jan McBarron story mentioned previously. When Jan chose to live a healthy self-image lifestyle, she initially could not list one thing as being a positive quality she had. That shows you where her self-image was at that particular time. Hopefully you have many qualities you can list that make you a very special and unique individual. If not, there is much hope ahead.

In all fairness, I should go ahead and tell the rest of Jan's story. When she started reading my book *See You at the Top,* she had been a nurse for six years. She weighed well over 200 pounds. She was a heavy smoker. And she decided that she wanted more out of life.

One day I was speaking in Atlanta, Georgia, and at the end of the session I was signing books. I noticed a lady and her husband seated there, waiting patiently. When I finished, she introduced herself. She said, "I'm Jan McBarron. I'm the one who wrote you the letter."

I said, "Yes, Jan. It's a delight to see you."

She said, "I decided life had more to offer. And now, what a delight it is to be able to say to you—it's Jan McBarron, MD."

She was motivated and went to medical school. She was the only nurse in the entire four years who was there. Almost no nurses ever move on into medical school. It's one of those rare things that occur. She worked full-time to support herself as a nurse working the night shift every night so she could go through medical school. As of this writing, Jan McBarron is one of four ladies in the United States who is a recognized specialist in bariatrics, or weight loss. She is slender. She's where she should be. She no longer smokes. She's reduced over 90 percent of her alcohol consumption. She runs marathons. She teaches the functionally illiterate how to read. She reads at least one good, positive, motivational book every month.

She is doing things that are absolutely, to her, incredible. They are the things you've been reading about throughout this book. Now, I don't know how that grabs you, but that says to me that anybody who can make that kind of progress can really give us all an inspiration to live by.

Step Fourteen. *Make a victory list of all of your past successes.* Jan said, again, that when she started her journey to a healthy self-image lifestyle, her successes in her mind had been so minimal that she listed such things as "I learned how to read" and "I learned how to go to school." But she said, "As I got more involved, I could add to that list and add to that list and add to that list."

Think of all the things you have done that you are proud of in your lifetime. Odds are great that there are an enormous number of things you can list. You passed a course that people thought was so difficult. You made a sale that there was no chance of making. You healed a relationship that was impossible to do. Make a list of all of the things that you have done—and when you make that list, review it regularly.

Step Fifteen. *Learn to* **love to read.** Dr. Alice C. Blair was the superintendent of the Chicago District 13 Manierre Elementary School, which is located in an underprivileged neighborhood. When she took that school over, only three of the eight hundred students were reading at grade level. Three years later, more than 50 percent of the students were reading at grade level. The progress continued. Dr. Blair said that "Ninety percent of all teen-age male delinquents read below the third-grade level."

I'm convinced that in the United States, public education and the government will never solve our illiteracy problem. I believe it's up to individuals like you and me and businesses to go out of our way and start teaching people how to read.

What a tragic waste of resources in our society that we let so many people slip through the cracks. There's nothing that will give you the satisfaction as great as teaching the functionally illiterate how to read and then teaching them to learn to love to read.

Step Sixteen. *Get in shape.* It's amazing how much better you feel when you're in good shape physically. There's a beautiful book written by Peter Strudwick entitled *Come Run with Me.* The book is about a lot more than running. When Peter Strudwick was born, he had no feet. His mother had contracted German measles while she was pregnant, which caused his deformity. All Peter had were stumps to run on, but he ran over 20,000 miles. He completed the Pikes Peak Marathon on at least three different occasions. He's never won a race, but he's never lost one—because the fact that he runs and always finishes says a great deal about being a winner. Get in shape. It does wonders for your self-image.

Step Seventeen. *Learn some manners.* John T. Molloy, author of the book *Dress for Success,* says that 30 percent of the people at the executive level who are interviewed at dinner for an executive position are turned down because they have such lousy manners. They do not know how to hold a knife and fork. They don't know what to do with a spoon after they put the sugar in the tea. They do not know where to place their napkin. They don't know any of those little niceties. If you do not know your manners or if your child does not know, I really encourage you to learn some manners as well as teach your children. Or enroll them in a course that teaches those things—because it does make a difference.

Step Eighteen. *Use your imagination.* Draw pictures of the person you want to be. Pick out role models, someone whom you admire, and use your imagination. Visualize yourself becoming possessed with all of the good qualities in that individual whom you want to emulate.

Many years ago in Brooklyn, a tour guide was taking a group of kids around the museum. At the very entrance to museum, there was a statue of a man who was a Greek athlete. When people looked at it, they assumed that it was just a statue. But, the tour director pointed out to the group, back in those days they always used an actual physical model and the statue was actually a replica, a duplicate, a reproduction of an athlete.

There was a skinny kid there named Angelo Siciliano and Angelo was intrigued with that bit of information. He said to the tour guide, "You mean that a human being can actually look that?" Here was a small-framed young kid looking at a statue of a muscular athlete. The tour

94

director said, "Yes. A live model actually posed for the artist who made the sculpture."

Well, they went on with the tour, and later they noticed Angelo was missing. They went back to the statue. There he was. He was still intrigued with all of the muscles and the physique of this individual. He started writing off to bodybuilding companies and asking them about the equipment so he could develop his muscles. But Angelo was penniless and those things cost lots of money.

But he was determined he was going to do something about his body and kept thinking about that model in his mind. That's the way he wanted to look.

He developed a process known as dynamic tension and his muscles started to grow. One day he and his buddies were up on the roof of one of the tenement buildings and they were playing around. All the kids had their shirts off and there was a statue up there. As they were playing, one of the kids said, "Well, look at Angelo and look at the statue. Angelo looks exactly like Atlas."

I'm talking about, of course, Charles Atlas, aka Angelo Siciliano, described by many as having the most beautiful, perfectly formed body since those Greek athletes all of those years ago. In his imagination, that's the way he saw them.

Step Nineteen. To build your self-image, we go back to the cause of a poor self-image, except this time we put it this way—*avoid pornography.* Avoid watching soap operas (and R and X-rated television shows or movies). Avoid reading horoscopes. All of those things have a detrimental impact in your mind. I want you to be so very conscious of what goes into that beautiful mind of yours that every time you start to read a book or look at a magazine or watch the television or see a video or movie, you will ask yourself, "Will reading or watching this contribute to my well-being? Will it lift me up—or will it put me down?" When you know it won't be uplifting or wholesome, toss the book and magazine, turn off the TV and video, and walk out of the movie theater. It's for your own good.

Step Twenty. *Learn from the successful failure.* Enrico Caruso was repeatedly told by his music teacher that he did not have the voice to be an opera singer. Every time he would try to hit the high notes, his voice would break. He was told, "You will never make it as a singer." (Caruso became extremely popular worldwide as an operatic tenor.) Until he was ten years old, Thomas Edison was considered to be a dunce. Brilliant scientist Albert Einstein and aerospace engineer Wernher von Braun both flunked courses in math when they were children.

Undoubtedly the greatest failure of the past century was baseball player Hank Aaron. Aaron struck out over 1,400 times, but most don't think of him as being much a failure. Do we? He hit 755 home runs and held the all-time record for many years, breaking Babe Ruth's record. Yet, the truth is, he struck out well over 1,400 times.

Most football fans don't think of Terry Bradshaw as being a failure because he took the Pittsburgh Steelers to four Super Bowls and won all four of them. Yet, as of the time of this writing, Terry Bradshaw threw more incomplete passes than 99.9 percent of all of the football players who will ever play the game. And most believe that Roger Staubach is a real hero. He is the good guy, the All-American for everybody. Staubach completed a lot of passes, but the truth is he too threw more incomplete passes than 99 percent of all of the football players who will ever play the game.

You can learn from successful failures.

You can learn from successful failures. You see, the difference between a big shot and a little shot is that a big shot is just a little shot who kept shooting. Keep shooting, friend, is what I'm saying.

Number Twenty-One. *Take a course in speaking—**public speaking**.* This will do more, faster for your self-image than any other single thing. *Reader's Digest* says that public speaking is the number-one fear of people in America. It is very natural to be uncomfortable speaking in front of an audience. But let me tell you something, there's nothing that will improve that self-image faster than a course in public speaking. Get involved in Toastmasters or Toast-mistresses. Get involved in a course that will let you stand up and express yourself in a community college class, in your church, community activities, or service clubs. Get involved. It will help you tremendously.

*Step Twenty-Two. If you need it, **get help.*** I don't know why, but in our society we still think that there is some deep, dark mystery and something a little weird and a little wrong to admit that we have some problems that we can't handle. We're reluctant in many cases to go to a counselor, somebody who is skilled and trained to give us direction and guidance. If you need some help, get it. It's amazing what it can do for you. If you broke your leg, you wouldn't hesitate a moment about calling a doctor. There are certain things with our minds that can get broken or go astray. When those things happen, get some help.

Step Twenty-Three. To improve your self-image, *look at yourself in the eye.* Look in the mirror and tell yourself that you're an honest, very intelligent, highly motivated, very enthusiastic, dependable—go right down the list of good qualities—individual. Some people won't even look themselves in the eye. When you look yourself in the eye, that's the first step. Step number two of step twenty-three is to learn to look children in the eye. They're nonthreatening. Later, you can move up to your peer group and learn to look them in the eye. Now, why is that so important? It is so important, friend, because you've heard it 10,000 times, "Don't trust anyone who won't look you in the eye."

98

Yet—the biggest con men I have ever known in my life could look a person dead center in the eye with those baby blues or dark browns and charm someone right out of their pocketbook. The fact that somebody looks you in the eye really does not have anything to do with their honesty, but the public perception is that it does. So, if you want to be accepted, if you want to make friends more easily, look people in the eye. It will gain friends and acceptance—and that does good things for your self-image.

A lot of people hesitate to look others in the eye because they fear the establishment of any kind of a relationship. Now, obviously, I'm not talking about flirting with somebody. I'm just talking about looking an individual in the eye as we do in our normal exchanges of life every day.

The last thing you do before you leave the house every morning is to get right in front of the mirror and say, "Remember, (state your name), God loves you and so do I." It'll make a difference in that image you see in the mirror.

Step Twenty-Four. Alter your physical appearance *if it is desirable.* When our youngest daughter was seventeen years old, I was startled to hear her say to her mother and me one day, "I'm concerned about my ears." Now, I thought my daughter was so very pretty—as pretty as our other two daughters and my wife. When I looked at this dear girl, I saw close to perfection. I had never noticed her ears. She said, "Daddy, haven't you ever noticed that I always have my hair over my ears?"

99

I said, "No, I'm afraid I haven't. I just thought that everything was fine."

She said, "Well look, Daddy, my ears stick out."

"Sweetheart, that's easy."

We went to a good plastic surgeon. It was a relatively simple operation. I didn't say inexpensive; I said simple. And when you see my youngest daughter today, I'll guarantee you she has her hair fixed so that you can see her ears. It is amazing what that did to her self-image.

I encourage you—if there is something you can do today that will improve your image, do it.

SUMMARY

All these steps are designed to help you *accept yourself.* When you do that, it will no longer be a matter of life or death for others to accept you. At that point, you will not only be accepted by them, they will actually seek you.

Accept yourself and believe you can be a champion at whatever you set your mind to.

The Japanese raise special trees—the Bonsai tree. It's small, usually about 18 inches, 20 inches, or 24 inches tall. It's a perfectly formed tree, but it's a miniature version. In the rich soil of California, there is another tree—a giant Sequoia. They call it the General Sherman. It reaches 275 feet up in the air and measures 36 feet in diameter at the base. Mathematicians have calculated that if they were to cut that tree down, there'd be enough lumber there to build thirty-five five-room houses. Interestingly enough, the Bonsai tree and the General Sherman at one time were the same size. Each weighed, when they were seeds, roughly 1/3000 of an ounce.

When the Bonsai tree stuck its head above the soil, they extracted it and tied off the feeder and some of the taproots and it made it a miniature tree. Beautiful, perfectly formed, but nevertheless a miniature. Its growth was stymied. The General Sherman fell into the rich soil of California. It was nurtured by the rains and the natural chemicals and the fertilizers that are naturally there in that soil, and it grew to be the giant that it is today.

It is my absolute conviction that we as human beings have the choice. We can stymie ourselves. We can tie off the taproots and the feeder roots and we can end up being a Bonsai tree. Or we can choose to flourish and nourish ourselves with the right inputs into our mind, take the steps we've been talking about, and decide to become the General Sherman in life. The choice really is yours. I hope and believe you've chosen to become the

101

General Sherman—standing tall and sturdy and becoming a natural champion.

You can be if you believe you can. Buy the ideas you've been reading about and follow the procedures prescribed. If you do, I'll see *you*—and yes I really do mean *you*—at the top.

CHAPTER 7

The Immensity of Relationships

Relationships are enormously important; they affect all ages, all colors, all beliefs, all creeds. We have to deal with both male and female interactions as well. I love what George Washington Carver had to say. This gentle, humble botanist once advised, *"How far you go in life depends on your being tender with the young, passionate with the aged, sympathetic with the striving, and tolerant of the weak and the strong, because someday in life you will have been all of these."*

That is so true.

Carver was one of the most unique men in the history of our country. He was a man who is forever recognized as being the founder of Tuskegee University. Carver said one day he was in prayer and he was saying, "God, I want to serve You, I want to do what You want me to do. I would like for You to reveal to me the mysteries of the universe." And according to Carver at that precise moment, a peanut fell at his feet. And the Lord spoke to him and he said, "George, the peanut is more your size."

He said it was a very interesting experience, but he decided to settle for the peanut instead of the universe. And he went on to discover 300 different uses of the peanut and 118 uses for the sweet potato. When you look at something like that, you can see tremendous opportunity even in a peanut.

We have more joy, more happiness, and more excitement in life because of proper relationships than any other factor.

What we're going to look at in this chapter is the tremendous opportunity inside the human being for good, healthy relationships. There's more misery, more frustration, anxiety, and grief because of improper relationships than any other single factor. However, we have more joy, more happiness, and more excitement in life because of proper relationships than any other factor.

Relationships obviously start at the beginning of life and continue to the end of life. Good or bad, relationships determine our effectiveness with our family, our friends, our associates, and with everyone else. Consequently, relationships are extraordinarily important—and having the proper attitude in our relationships is extremely important.

I believe this next little story sums it up quite well.

The story goes that a man was being given a chance to look at both Heaven and hell so he could make a decision as to which place he really wanted to go. So, they took him into the halls of hell first of all. And as he walked in, he thought to himself, *Boy now, if this is hell, this is for me.* What he saw was a large number of people seated at a very long banquet table. And, on the banquet table, there was every kind of food that you could possibly imagine. There were vegetables, salads, meats, all of the entrees, all of the desserts; there on the table in front of the people was every type of food that's available in this world today.

But as the man looked at the people who were sitting at the table there, he noticed that even though there was a feast in front of them, they appeared to be starved. As a matter of fact, there was no laughter, there was no joy, and nobody was having any fun at all. And yet, right in front of them was a feast that anybody would have loved to have had.

And then the man was taken into Heaven. And there he walked in and he saw the identical long banquet table in front of him on which were the same magnificently delicious-looking foods, exactly the same menu as it been in hell. But this time he noticed that these people were all laughing and singing and having a marvelous time. They were well fed; they were healthy.

The visitor who was taking the tour turned to his guide and said, "Well, I'm a little puzzled. As a matter of fact, I'm very puzzled. I could not help but notice that the people had the same menu, the same food as in the other place...but over there they were starving. Over here, in reality they're having a wonderful time. They're well fed, they're healthy. What on earth is the difference?"

And the tour guide said, "Well, had you looked very carefully, you would've noticed that in both places there is a knife and a fork strapped to the arms of each one of the inhabitants. And, the knife and the fork are both four feet long. Over in hell they're trying to feed themselves, but they cannot. But in Heaven they are feeding the person directly in front of them, who in turn is feeding them."

It is true that you can have everything in life you want if you help enough other people get what they want.

That pretty well sums up the gist if what I'll be talking about. Because you see, it is true that you can have everything in life you want if you help enough other people get what they want.

WHAT EVERYONE WANTS IN LIFE

As we look at relationships, let's very quickly review what everyone wants in life. Everyone wants to be *happy*, everyone wants to be *healthy*, everyone wants to be at least *reasonably prosperous*, everyone wants to have *friends*, everyone wants to have *peace of mind*, everyone wants to be *secure*.

Now for those who have families, they obviously want to have *good family relationships*. As we look at the six basics that everybody wants, let's look at the role that relationships play. All of the authorities will tell you that your health, to a very large degree, depends on how well you get along with other people. Everybody will agree that how happy you are depends, to a very large degree, on your relationships with other people. Many will tell you that your amount of prosperity is determined, to a large degree, by how well you get along with others.

Your amount of prosperity is determined, to a large degree, by how well you get along with others.

Ohio State University, as a simple example, did a study of the fifty reasons why people lose their jobs. And they had to get to reason number sixteen before it had anything to do with their technical expertise or their job skills. *The first fifteen reasons dealt with attitudes and their ability to cooperate with, get along with others.* Your relationships certainly will determine the number and quality of friends you have. Your relationships will determine, to a large degree, just how much satisfaction and peace of mind you have. Your relationships will determine just how secure you are, because the most insecure feeling in the world is to know that you have no one who really loves and cares for you.

The most secure feeling is having good family relationships. Every time I see anyone who is ill, the first thing they talk about is whether they are alone or whether their friends and family have been supportive of them. Of course, the key to good family relationships is the way you get along with those people.

This chapter includes lots of stories, parables, examples, analogies, and quotations. As always, I'll identify the source of my information when possible. I do always identify the source for three basic reasons: number one, it is the right thing to do; number two, it indicates to a degree that I've done my research; and number three, in the event it is wrong, I can always say, "You know that fellow should've known better than that. Or I can't believe that lady didn't know any better than that."

IT'S ALL ABOUT RELATIONSHIP

Psychologist Renee Fuller has discovered that storytelling is the key to learning. People remember stories; and if the story has a real moral to it, a real lesson in it, then we will remember the lesson.

As a sales trainer, for example, I do a one-hour session on one single sales story that I spent no more than twenty minutes in the entire transaction, and yet there are twenty-five specific lessons that I extract from that one story that took place from a sales training, sales presentation point of view. And people remember it simply because they can identify with the story.

Let me share another story, which had considerable influence in my life and it emphasizes again why storytelling is such an effective method of teaching.

During World War II, one of my dreams was to become a naval aviator. Oh, I was really gung-ho. I was turning seventeen on a Saturday, and the following Monday I signed up or started trying to sign up to join the Air Force. I was ready to go.

Now, between the eleventh and twelfth grade, I realized that I needed more math and more science if I was going to make it into the naval air corp. I was not an outstanding student, and I well remember the time I bought home four F's and a C. My mother was understandably upset, and she said, "Son, I just don't understand this. You bring home these four F's and then this C. What on earth happened?" I said, "Well, Mom, obviously I just spent too much time concentrating on that one subject."

Maybe it wasn't quite that bad, but I was not an outstanding student. Anyway, I attended summer school between the eleventh and twelfth grade because I was so gung-ho about getting into the Air Force and I had to have more math and science.

In order to graduate, one of the courses I had to take was American History. I had to learn it. Well naturally, I didn't want to take a history class, because it obviously was going to do me no good. What possible benefit would

I gain by learning about something that happened one hundred years ago, two hundred years ago, or three hundred years ago? I wanted to get on with the matter at hand. I wanted to learn how to fly airplanes so I could go shoot down the enemy and win the war. That was my goal.

So, I walked into the classroom that day determined I was going to learn all I needed to know...about getting out of that class. In reality, I walked in with a chip on my shoulder, which indicates that there's wood up above.

I walked in and saw that Coach Joby Harris was the teacher. For the first session, the coach threw all of us a curve. All he did was sell. I happen to believe that everything is selling. He sold each one of us on why we had to learn history. Before he got through, I was a history major; as a matter of fact, it was the only course I consistently made A's in while I was in college.

Toward the end of that first class, he shifted gears. He started talking about America's future and where it lay. He said to us, "If those of you who have an ability that goes beyond just earning a living and providing for your own needs and the needs of your family—if you have that kind of an ability, you must devote some of your time, effort, and resources to help those people who have less skill and less opportunity and less ability than you have."

Coach Harris said, "As a matter of fact, if we do not reach down and start lifting these people up with better education, better direction, better opportunity, and better motivation—if we don't start lifting them up, the day will come when they will reach up and by the sheer weight of numbers will start pulling us down."

Coach Harris was a prophet, considering the millions of people today on welfare. The millions of illiterate people. The millions who have catastrophic diseases. Our resources are being depleted and the country is literally being pulled down. As of this writing, this generation will be the first generation in our country's history that will have a lower standard of living than the preceding one.

HELP ENOUGH OTHER PEOPLE

Everything our company does is built on the basic concept that you can have everything in life you want if you help enough other people get what they want. The work we do in prisons and schools, churches and drug rehab centers, and our other efforts to help others get their start is right there in our primary business belief.

Coach Harris obviously had a dramatic impact on my life. When he was a youngster, he was a Boy Scout and his Scout Master was Thomas B. Abernathy. Mr. Abernathy was the first Scout official in the entire state of Mississippi in addition to having his own individual Scout troop. For whatever reason, Mr. Abernathy took an interest in "little Joby Harris." He became like a second father to him. Though Joby had a father, Mr. Abernathy taught him not only scouting, but many other things about living an honorable and honest life.

Mr. Abernathy had four children—three daughters and a son. The youngest daughter was named Jean, and Jean Abernathy has been Mrs. Zig Ziglar for more than forty-one years. Now, there's no way on earth that Mr. Abernathy could've known that when he was spending that extra time with little Joby Harris, that he was developing the boy and helping him form his philosophy of life and that this boy would later have such a dramatic impact on his future son-in-law's life, which made him a better husband and a better father to the grandchildren, which he never had the privilege of seeing.

In relationships, what I'm saying is, we never really know just how far we're going to influence not only that life or someone else's life. We need to be very careful in how we handle our relationships, as they may have far-reaching impact.

HONESTY, NOT SCARE TACTICS

I so vividly recall that in contrast to this wonderful generational influence, there is another one of my World War II stories with a much different result of an influential relationship.

The government put us into the military service, then we were put in college to get us ready for going to flight school. The first day in my college English class, I heard that the teacher there was reputed to be the toughest teacher anywhere under any circumstances. She truly was a big lady, about six feet, two inches tall, had shoulders like a linebacker, and she really was an imposing physical specimen.

They said that she was an absolute genius on the subject of English. She knew it better than anybody in the entire state. When she walked into the classroom that first day, she looked at the class and said, "Class, I'm your teacher. I want to tell you something about me so you'll know what to expect."

She said, "I have been in this institution over twenty-five years, and during those twenty-five years, there has only ever been one student who made an A. I can absolutely assure you that will never happen again. That was an accident, it just slipped by, it will not take place again. Not only that," she said, "but, as I look at you, you might as well know in advance, I think it's only fair to warn you that fully one-third of you will not even pass this course."

Now, I want you to get the scene. We were youngsters from all over the country gathered together at this college for the purpose of getting ready to be full-time members of the military. Most of us had a lifetime dream of serving our country as aircraft flyers. Our entire career depended upon passing English and all other courses. One failure and we would be out—the competition was enormously tough.

I heard somebody in the back say, "Boy, she is one tough lady." And somebody else said, "Yeah, but she really knows her English." Now that I have no doubts about, she knew her English—but she didn't know her students, and she didn't know her psychology.

No matter what you do— communications and relationships are always going to be involved.

We were already scared to death. I just wonder how many more guys would've passed the class had she walked in and said, "Gentlemen, I might as well tell you. This is a tough class. But I might also tell you that I am a very competent instructor. I love English, and I love my students, and I just want you to know in advance that I'm going to give it my very best. I am going to teach you what I know about the English language, and about the subject, we're going to dig into it in depth. If for any reason any of you fail, I just want you to know in advance it is going to be your fault and not mine. I'm committed to teach the most effective course I've ever taught—for your benefit."

I believe that type of declaration would've been infinitely, definitely better than the gloom and doom she predicted.

You see, what I really question is if she really was a competent English teacher. When she stands up and says that only one student has ever made an A and one-third of the students won't pass the class—I wonder if she wasn't really saying, "I'm not really very good at teaching the subject. I know the subject, but I can't teach it."

I accept full responsibility in my communication with other people—whether one on one or in front of a large audience. If I do not communicate clearly, it is not your fault. I've always believed when somebody is speaking or teaching, if I don't understand, it's their fault. And the reason I say that, I believe anybody who understands their subject matter will be able to figure out a way to present it to me in such a manner that if I work, and if I accept my responsibility of learning and paying attention and really digging into it, then if I do not learn I believe the teacher has to carry the major share of the responsibility.

I want you to know that I accept that responsibility. I believe and believe strongly that out of this book, you're going to get a tremendous amount of information that will make you more effective in whatever you do. No matter what you do—communications and relationships are always going to be involved.

Now we're going to concentrate on our ability and the importance of looking for the good.

SEE THE GOOD IN PEOPLE

A study was done in New York City a number of years ago on the self-made millionaires there. They selected one hundred of these wealthy people, and as they did this study, they discovered that the millionaires had tremendously varied backgrounds. They ranged in age from early twenties to the late seventies; they ranged in educational background from one having only completed the fifth grade to one person who had earned two PhD degrees. Something like 60 percent or 70 percent came from towns of less than 15,000 people, for whatever that means.

But what the researchers found that was *absolutely consistent* in each of these self-made millionaires—what they each had in common—was that every one of them had *the ability to see the good in other people and in situations.*

We need to be good-finders and encouragers.

So, if we really start understanding that we need to be good-finders and encouragers, then we've learned a very important lesson.

The story is told of a businessman who went down to catch the subway, and he was in kind of a hurry. There was a beggar at the entrance to the subway selling pencils. The businessman reached in his pocket and pulled out a dollar that he dropped into the tray where the pencils were and hurried to get on the subway.

But after he got on the subway car, he still had a minute or so before it was to leave, so he got back off, went over to the beggar selling the pencils, and said, "You know, I owe you an apology, I was in such a hurry that I forgot. You're selling a good product, fully worth the price. You're a businessman just like I am. I'll take my two pencils."

Many months later at a social event, the businessman encountered there a well-dressed young man who came up to him and said, "There's no way on earth you would ever recognize me. But," he said, "many months ago I was selling pencils in the subway station and you gave me my dignity. You did not treat me like a beggar. You treated me like a businessman. I want to say, thank you."

I wonder how many beggars, if they would be treated like businessmen and women, would not be beggars today.

IT'S IMPORTANT TO BE NICE

Somebody said once, "It's nice to be important, but it's more important to be nice." I believe that's true.

One of the most significant events of my first year in Dallas, Texas was the meeting of a man who since has come to be a very close friend of mine. His name is Walter Haley; he at that time was in the insurance business. He had conceived a new idea, which was selling insurance to the independent grocers around America via selling them as they bought and dealt with the warehouse. In other words, these monstrous warehouses, when they would bill the groceries to the independent grocers all over the country. Mr. Haley gave them the idea of billing them for their insurance for all of the employees. I'm talking about life insurance as well as health and accident insurance.

Walter's average salesperson was selling 10, 15, 20 million dollars' worth of whole life insurance. That was the range in those days, whereas the average of life insurance agent was selling in the neighborhood of about $1 million, and it took a pretty good one to sell a million dollars.

A friend of mine had said, "I want you to meet Walter Haley; he is the most unusual man." Well, you know how some people have a certain chemistry that when you meet them it seems like you've been friends for life? Well, Walter Haley has that charisma about him; when you meet him, you want to get to know him better. When initially introduced to him, Walter Haley stuck out his hand, and the first thing he said was, "Zig, I've been hearing about you. Man, I am just flattered that you would come over to see me. And I can't wait to show you around and let you see what's going on."

We walked into a warehouse and I was stunned. I didn't know there was that much food in the world, much less under one roof. As we walked in, Walter said, "Excuse me one second, Zig." He walked over to the switchboard operator and said, "I'm Walter Haley and I just want to tell you that I think you're doing an absolutely magnificent job on this switchboard."

Then he said to the switchboard operator, "I never dial this number that I don't get the distinct impression that all you're doing is sitting there waiting for me to call so you can put me through to the proper person." He said sincerely, "You do a beautiful job."

The operator said, "Why thank you, Mr. Haley, I really appreciate that."

He said, "Well, I appreciate you."

We turned and walked down one of the corridors, and Walter says to me, "Excuse me a second, Zig." He stepped into the office and stuck his hand out toward the man standing there and said, "I haven't met you, I'm Walter Haley. I haven't had the privilege of even seeing you before. But I've been reading the reports and watching what's happening since you took over." And he said, "Man, you're just doing an absolutely magnificent job and I want to thank you for it."

The man smiled of course very broadly and said, "I do the best I can."

And Walter Haley said, "That's good enough for me. You just keep it up, you're really doing a marvelous job."

We left there, walked upstairs and into Walter's office. The first person we saw was his secretary, and he said, "Zig, shake hands with the greatest secretary who ever sat behind a desk."

And he said to her, "You know, my wife thinks you hung the moon, and she thinks you can take it down just whenever you want to, and I'm going to ask you to please leave it up there. I love to see it as I'm driving, especially on my way down south at night."

"Oh, Mr. Haley." She said, "You're always saying something like that, and your wife is really a sweet lady, but I just want you to know, keep it up, I really like to hear it."

We walked into his office and there sat an insurance rep. Walter said, "Zig, shake hands with one of the greatest life insurance men to ever put on a pair of shoes."

The rep said, "Oh Walter, you're always saying things like that. But I love it, I just love it."

Now, the entire trip took less than ten minutes. But do you believe that as a result of that ten minutes those four people had a marvelous day? Absolutely! He built them up one by one with his encouraging and uplifting comments.

Now, I want to stress something very important. Because this is the key. If you're *sincere*, it's enormously effective. If you're *insincere*, it's manipulative. A manipulator will say and do things so that he or she can win—and that's not what being a natural champion is all about. It's about seeing the good in others and revealing that to them.

If you're sincere, it's enormously effective. If you're insincere, it's manipulative.

Walter Haley, a multi, multi, multimillionaire, has friends everywhere he goes. He's what we call a happy-miser. He saves every friend he makes. He believes you can never get ahead by trying to get even. I think he's right.

The motivator understands that it's a win-win situation. You're not being kind for your benefit, you do it for their benefit, but when they benefit you benefit, and we go right back to the whole concept that you can have everything in life you want if you help enough other people get what they want.

CHAPTER 8

Lessons Learned

The question is, how do you treat people?

This question might shock you a little bit, but the answer may shock you more. I believe that you ought to treat people like cows.

I was raised in Yazoo City, Mississippi. And when I was a child there, we survived because we had five milk cows and a large garden. My mother taught us many, many lessons during those growing up years—our dad had died early in life—but I can tell you something about cows.

If you walk into a cold barn on a freezing winter morning, and an old cow's lying there, and you walk over and give her kick and say, "Get up! No wonder your milk production and butter fat is down. You're just lying around.

Did you hear what I said? Get up! You're going to have to do a better job of producing."

Now, if you treat that old cow like that, let me tell you, first of all, she just might kick you back. Second, I can empathically tell you that the milk she produces will be less in amount—it will be unfit for human consumption. And, you will get her so upset, this is a fact, that the milk will be too bitter for anyone to drink.

Now I don't necessarily think to get sweet, delicious milk that you have to walk in the barn and hug the old cow, and say, "Good morning, Old Cow," though it's not going to hurt you to at least give her a little hug. You can look at her and say, "My goodness, you've got the best-looking pair of double legs I think I have seen today. And your coat is so nice and soft. I just want to tell you, Old Cow, how proud I am of you. You know, your production is way up and your butter fat is rising steadily, and I have an idea that today you're going to make your best effort ever to break all your records. I just really appreciate you, Old Cow."

Now you might be thinking, *Ziglar, that's pretty far-fetched.* Well, let me tell you a true story—with a lesson learned.

Back in the 1930s, a cow that produced three gallons of milk was considered a standard producer. In the 1980s, a three-gallon producer would be a candidate for hamburger. She really would. From the '30s to the '80s, there has been some marvelous progress in dairy farming.

What we did in those lean years, my mother would buy cows. She would buy the average producing, the three-gallon producers. And first of all my mother would give the cow a little more feed—she would feed her better. Second, she would give the cow a name. And third, she would treat that old cow lovingly and gently. And if one of us boys mistreated one of her cows, as we would say down home, it is just too wet to plow, which meant we were in bad trouble.

The way you treat people absolutely makes a significant, positive difference.

Within six months after we brought a cow home, that cow was up to a four-gallon-a-day producer. And invariably, within a year, that cow was producing close to five gallons a day. A dramatic increase in productivity. Mother would then sell that cow and get as much as $50 more than she had paid for it. Oftentimes, or always, she got at least $25 more. Now, the 1980s, when you talk about another $25 or $50, you're not talking about anything.

But let me tell you, during the 1930s, you could buy one pound of what they call streak o' lean, streak o' fat, or salt pork for seven cents. Three pounds of the best bacon sold for 27 cents. So when talking about another $25 or $50, you're talking about a substantial increase in the standard of living.

The way we treated that old cow made a significant, positive difference—and the way you treat people absolutely makes a significant, positive difference as well.

BE KIND

We have a three-day school we call Born to Win. People literally come from all around the world to attend—to learn. Years ago in one of the sessions, a beautiful young black woman from Chicago attended the training. She looked like a beauty queen, she acted like a queen, she talked like a queen. She had a graceful manner about her that was really fascinating. She had a voice that was totally feminine, and yet so strong that 200 people in a room could hear her without any kind of amplifying system.

This woman was very a successful businesswoman who had, I believe at that time, 125 people working for her. Had you asked me, "Who in this class has got it all together? Who is completely successful? Who has the whole package? Which one of these people would you choose?" Without any hesitation I would've said, "The businesswoman from Chicago is the one I choose—the person who fits that description."

On Saturday afternoon, as we were ending the session, the woman came to me and asked, "Can I speak with you for a moment, privately?"

I said, "Well, of course."

As we chatted, she started to cry. She said, "You know what? In my lifetime, you're the first human being who's ever looked me right in the eye and said, 'You're important. I love you. God loves you.' That's why I came here… to hear those words from somebody who cared. I'll never forget this experience."

The greatest lesson I learned was that if you treat everybody like they're hurting, you'll be treating the vast majority of people in the proper way to ease the hurt. Relationships are so important.

My friend, Fred Smith, who's truly one of the brightest men I know, wrote a beautiful book entitled *You and Your Network*. He said:

> In those experiences in life where we encounter people who are rude and mean and nasty and ugly to us—and that's going to happen in lots and lots of cases—when those things happen, what you have to understand is that they're not trying to hurt you when they're mean and rude and nasty and ugly. In 99 percent of the cases they're that way because they are hurting.

If we can understand that, it will take the sting out of the words or situation. Let's say we're a salesperson who just failed to get the appointment, or failed to make the sale, maybe our prospect invites us to leave as quickly as possible, or we're in a management-employee situation and we feel like the manager has been too hard on us, or we're in a peer situation and our peer was insulting—it is so very helpful in building winning relationships if we understand that they don't really want to hurt us, they're actually hurting themselves. They're defensive and lash out.

If everybody was like my good friend Tom Hatfield, this book you're reading, *You're a Natural Champion,* would not have even been necessary. Tom is our insurance representative and has been a good friend for quite a while. A while ago there was a big storm here in Dallas, Texas. Our home is centrally heated, but everybody here, and especially old Zig, just loves fireplaces. Oh, I love to watch that wood burn in that fireplace. Of all the times to run completely out of wood, old Zig ran completely out of wood during the storm.

I knew that Tom knows about everybody in town, so I got on the telephone and said, "Tom, who do you know that I can call to bring me a load of wood?"

He said, "Well, Zig, I don't know right off the top of my head, but I'll scout around and see what I can find."

About an hour later my doorbell rang. I went to the front door and there was Tom Hatfield. He said, "Zig, I brought you some wood. We have more than we need at the moment and we're going to be getting another load next month, anyhow." He brought me enough wood to last us three or four days, maybe even five or six days of steadily burning wood.

You might say, "Well, Zig, that's just a good salesman looking after his client." I'll acknowledge there might be a degree of truth in there. But I fervently believe that had I never bought a dime's worth of anything from Tom Hatfield, he would've brought that wood because he and I are friends.

LIVE THE GOLDEN RULE

What does going a little bit out of your way for someone else do to your relationships? I believe that's the key. The Bible says in a lot of different ways that the best human relations rule of all is to "Do unto others as you would have them do unto you." In other words, "Treat others like you want them to treat you." It's just so very, very simple—yet so very, very important.

There's another verse in the Bible that says, "Be kind to one another, tenderhearted, forgiving each other." This admonition is enormously important in our scheme of things today. Isn't it? There's another verse that says to go the extra mile. As mentioned previously, if somebody demands your cloak, give your coat also. If they demand that you go one mile, go the second mile with them.

Remember, you can have everything in life you want, if you help enough other people get what they want. That's the bottom line that I keep repeating. But does it work? Let's look at that question more closely by considering two things.

Number one, you are *what* you are and *where* you are because of what has gone into your mind so far in your lifetime. You can *change what* you are and you can *change where* you are by changing what goes into your mind.

Number two, I remind you that life is tough. I don't care what you do, whether you're a household executive, a salesperson, a manager, a schoolteacher, a physician, a minister—it doesn't matter what you do, life can be tough. But when you're tough on yourself by keeping true to moral and character standards and living the Golden Rule, life is infinitely easier on you.

A GOOD RELATIONSHIP CONCEPT

What is a good relationship concept? I believe that Bear Bryant had one of the greatest relationship concepts that I've ever heard of. During his twenty-five-year tenure as the coach of the University of Alabama's football team, he won six national championships and thirteen conference championships. Coach Bryant had a basic philosophy that if things went badly for his team, he'd always say, "Well, it's all my fault."

I have seen when his team was just obliterated. I mean, wiped out. The other team being two or three touchdowns ahead, and always in the interview Bryant would say, "Well, you've just got to face it. They just simply outcoached me. The other coach did a better job of getting his team ready."

Bryant's relationships concept? If it was a bad outcome, he said it was his fault. If it was mediocre, he would say, "Well, it was kind of a team effort there. Me and the team together, we just did a mediocre job." But if it was a fantastic win, he would always say, "I've got to tell you, this is the greatest group of young men I've ever had the privilege of coaching. They did it!"

Friend, that concept will work every time to build important relationships. I don't care where or what or who you are.

Losers are basically described in the following little parable by Charles Allen in his book *The Miracle of Love*. He says that a fisherman told him that when you're crabbing, when you're catching crabs, you don't need to put a top on the basket where you will be keeping the crabs. All you need is an open basket because, "When you put the second crab in there, any time one tries to climb up, the other one will reach up and pull it down."

Those are losers. Those are the people who are so insecure that they cannot really relate to somebody else being successful. They think that if somebody is being successful, it means they've got to be put down. They believe in the seesaw principle, "The only way I'm going to go up is to put somebody else down." But if you notice, the seesaw is always up and down and up and down. And people who have that philosophy are going to be up and down, and mostly down.

The best exercise is to reach down and lift someone up.

It's always been true that the best exercise is to reach down and lift someone up. It's also true that when you go *looking* for friends, you're not likely to find them. But when you go out to *be* a friend, you'll find them everywhere—because what you send out does come back.

When you go out wanting to be a friend, you'll find them everywhere.

I know you've probably heard this story but it's worth another telling. A little boy and his mother had a blowup one morning, and in a fit of anger, as small children often do, the boy said to his mother, "I hate you! I hate you!" Then realizing what he had said and fearing for his future comfort, he made a mad dash out the front door. They lived on the side of a hill, and when he got out there, he was still frustrated and bent out of shape, so he started screaming, "I hate you! I hate you!" Then the echo came back, "I hate you. I hate you."

It frightened the little boy and he ran inside. He said, "Mom, there's a mean little boy out there in the valley who says he hates me."

And his mother says, "Yes, but there's also another real nice little boy out there who loves you. You go out there and tell him that you love him."

So the little boy ran out, he yelled, "I love you! I love you!"

And the echo came back, "I love you. I love you."

Simple but true that what you send out comes back. Bottom line, does the concept work? Answer, yes, the concept works.

Years ago, Barry Tacker in Bay City, Texas was a disciplinarian at the school. They bought this basic idea that we're discussing and started teaching these concepts. If you're not a Texan, your state might not have disciplinarians nowadays, but as you may guess, the disciplinarian is not the most popular member of the teaching staff. As a matter of fact, just the mention of the disciplinarian may instill fear in the minds of the students. When the teacher says, "Go see the disciplinarian," I'll tell you, the students froze, because they knew they were in trouble.

The first day this took place, a young fellow walked in, and the teacher said to him, "Mr. Tacker wants to see you." The youngster immediately became defensive. "I didn't do anything. I didn't do a thing!"

The teacher said, "Well, Mr. Tacker wants to see you right now before class starts." With fear and trembling, the young man went to see him. He walked in protesting, "Mr. Tacker, I didn't do a thing! Didn't do a thing!"

Mr. Tacker said, "Now, that's not what I heard."

"I didn't do it, Mr. Tacker! I didn't do it! I'm telling you, I didn't do it. I'm innocent!"

Mr. Tacker said, "Well, the story I got was this—this very morning, less than two blocks from here, you were seen helping an elderly lady across the street. Now, the question is, do you plead guilty or do you plead innocent?"

And enormously relieved, the young man said, "I did it, Mr. Tacker, I did it!"

Mr. Tacker said, "Does your mother have any idea what you're up to these days?"

The young man says, "Well, I don't guess so. I never told her."

Mr. Tacker said, "It's important that your mother knows, and I'm going to send this note home for her to sign. And I mean you'd better have her sign it and bring it back."

The youngster, of course, was elated. Hundreds of cases that year took place as they looked for things the students were doing right and they sent word home to the parents. The teachers, the school administrators, the students, and the parents all drew closer together because they understood that they were working on the same project. They were building champions.

ON THE SAME SIDE

Then there's the story of the little guy who was confronted by the three bullies, any one of whom could have obliterated him—and it looked like they were going to do exactly that. But this smart little fellow took a stick and he drew a line there on the ground and he backed up a few paces. He looked up at the biggest bully and said, "Now, you just step across that line." Well, with a confident expression, the big bully stepped across the line. The little guy said, "Now, we're both on the same side."

I wonder how many marriages would be better if the husbands and the wives clearly understand that they are both on the same side. I wonder how many school systems would be better if parents and students and teachers and administrators all understand they're on the same side. I wonder how much more productive we would be in our business environment if labor and management, employer, employee, all clearly understood that they are on the same side. That unless there is productivity, unless there is profit, then everybody there will be losers.

One of the most amazing stories I think I have ever heard is this one. Several years ago in Indianapolis, Indiana, a fellow named Charlie Fluger came to one of our seminars for educators. He bought into this concept, this idea of becoming a good-finder, seeking the best in people. He was the assistant principal at an inner-city school in Indianapolis, and this was to be their last year. I don't know how much you know about inner-city schools and the attitude that takes place any time a school is going to be closing down. When that school gets ready to close, everybody closes it about a year early. Why bother to take care of anything? You know, this is the last year, we might as well just let it go.

Well, Charlie Fluger went in with this basic idea of being a good-finder. He initiated a program called I Can. He made up little disks the size of a silver dollar and on each he wrote the words, "I can." Every time a youngster was voluntarily seen picking up a piece of paper, one of the teachers would give the student an I Can medal. If students were seen erasing the blackboard without being told, they received an I Can. If they turned in something that had been lost, they received an I Can. If they voluntarily welcomed a new student to school, they received an I Can. Anything helpful earned them an I Can.

136

When they received 100 I Cans, then each student was given a winner's t-shirt, an I Can T-shirt. With a school attendance of 592 kids, 587 of them received I Can t-shirts. Charlie said the I Cans got to be the badge of honor. It was a status symbol for the students to wear their I Can t-shirt. He said it even got to be a bit ridiculous. If there was a piece of paper blowing across the school yard, there'd quickly be five kids out there running after it. He said they helped elderly ladies cross the street…who didn't want to cross the street. And when a new youngster would come to school, about 300 kids would individually shake hands with him or her and welcome the new student to the school. There was never anything lost that was not found.

You might say, "Yeah, but 587 t-shirts? Isn't that rather expensive?" Yeah. Until you understand that there was not one single act of vandalism the whole year. Not a single drug arrest. Not a single drug bust. And teachers and parents and students and administrators came together more than they'd ever come together in that school.

A relationships approach in life works.

Now, friend, I'm talking about a relationships approach in life that works. Everybody becomes the winner. You've got to understand that when we say you can have everything in life you want, if you just help enough other people get what they want, we're talking about a philosophy, not manipulation. That's very important for you to understand.

CHAPTER 9

Response Equates to Treatment

I want to emphasize a point: the first responsibility of business is to make a profit. That's the first responsibility. And why is that? Very simple. If the business does not make a profit, it goes bankrupt, and if it goes bankrupt, every employee, including owners and managers, will be unemployed. Therefore, profit-making is extremely important.

Management psychologist James G. Carr adds a little twist to business. Businesses are focused on the bottom line—at least that's the reputation a whole lot of people seem to have. But James Carr has this to say when you are dealing with your employees, and it's a variation of the "look for the good" concept we've talked so much about. His concept is this: you don't go around looking for things to catch your employees doing. He says *go around looking for things you can help them do better with directions and encouragement.* That is the important thing. One more time—when you treat people exactly like you see them, they respond according to the way they're treated.

When you treat people exactly like you see them, they respond according to the way they're treated.

One of the best-known experiments ever conducted along these lines was done at Harvard University a number of years ago. Dr. Robert Rosenthal conducted a series of experiments with some rats. He took three groups of his students and three groups of rats on this experiment. He went to the first group of students and said, "Now, you are very, very fortunate. You have the super bright rats. These rats are the brightest rats known to man. They're going to be going down that maze in nothing flat. They're going to be eating more cheese than you can possibly imagine. You better lay in an extra supply of cheese."

Then Dr. Rosenthal went to the second group of students and he said, "You all have the average rats, not too bright, not too dumb, just a bunch of average rats. You better buy some cheese, though, because some of them will figure out a way to get through the maze."

To the third group of students he says, "Now, you have a problem. These are the dummies. These rats have been inbred for so many generations that they are sad beyond belief. It will be a miracle if any one of them ever finds the end of the maze. Oh, one of them might stumble, stutter, stagger, and eventually get there, but you'll know it's purely an accident."

During the next six weeks, under the most carefully controlled scientific conditions, they conducted the experiments. And just like Dr. Rosenthal had said, those bright rats went right down to the end of the maze, they ate lots of cheese, and they gained weight.

The average rats? Well, what do you expect from a bunch of average rats? They reached the end of the maze, some of them, but they didn't break any records, and all of them never did make it.

The idiot rats, oh, the dummies, they were really sad. Once in a while, one of them would stumble and stutter and stagger and fall down at the end of the maze, but they knew it purely was an accident.

Well, now the interesting thing is that there were no genius rats. There were no idiot rats. They were all out of the same litter, as a matter of fact. The rats were identical. The results were different because even the students, though they could not say to the rats, "Now, you're a dummy and you're a genius," they couldn't say those things; but nevertheless, in their own attitude, somehow or other it was communicated to the rats.

Let me ask you a question. What kind of kids do you have? What kind of neighbors do you have? What kind of employees do you have? You might say, "Ziglar, you're talking about those rats one minute and my kids the next. You gotta slow it down and draw me a little clearer picture, all right?" Will do.

Dr. Rosenthal and his students took the experiment a step further. They went to a school and said to the teacher, "You're in luck. You have the genius kids. Oh, are they ever so bright. Now, some of them are just a tad bit lazy and they're going to say, 'Teacher, don't give me too much. I just can't get all of that done!' And some of them are going to say, 'Wait a minute, we don't have the background for this.' But listen, you put it on them. These kids can do the work."

They went to the second teacher and said to her, "You've got a bunch of average kids. They're not too bright, they're not too dumb. They're just average kids and we would expect average results to come from them."

One year later, the "bright" kids were one full year ahead of the "average" kids, and of course you know the end of the story already, don't you? There were no bright kids. They were all average kids, but somehow, when we communicate that degree of expectancy, things begin to happen.

David Kerns, chairman of the board for Xerox, returned from this twenty-fifth trip to Japan. He said the major difference right now between what is happening there and what is happening in the U.S. is the word "expectancy." What do we expect from our kids? What do we expect from our employees? What do we expect for ourselves?

EXPECT THE BEST

While reading these previous few paragraphs, I hope your mate got more attractive and brighter, that your kids got smarter, that your employees got more productive and that their intelligence went up a few notches—because if they did not all have an increase from what you just read and has been proven, then they have a problem. And the problem, of course, is you.

The way we see people and treat people is so enormously important.

Let me give you an example within the family. Do you perhaps have three children or you're one of three children and maybe you are the middle child? There's something special about the middle child. They don't have the security of being the oldest, nor do they get all of the love and attention and affection of being the youngest. The middle child is just kind of stuck there.

When our third child was born, we knew we were going to have trouble with our second one. Sure enough, the first day when we brought our baby home, because of the input we had had from our friends and relatives and neighbors and complete strangers, we were all ready. We were set, we were prepared, we knew that middle child was going to be a problem for us, and it started the first day the baby arrived home from the hospital.

The friends and relatives and neighbors started coming to visit. The first thing they did was make a beeline for the bassinet to see that new baby. And you know what people always do with a new baby? "Oh, isn't she cute? Coocha coocha coocha! My, look how she holds her head up." They always say, "Look how she holds her head up." I don't know why they can't think of something else to say, but they always say that. Every baby I've ever seen in my life, they always say, "Look at the way...."

Well anyhow, the visitors just oogled and ogled the baby. Then they went over to the oldest daughter and said, "My, you sure are a big girl. I bet you're a lot of help to Mommy, aren't you? Can I take your baby sister home with me?" Well, what about that oddball stuck off over there in the middle? "Hi there." That was about the extent of it.

Yeah, like I say, we knew we were going to have trouble with Cindy and she did not disappoint us in the least. She became a griper and a whiner and a complainer. And old dad, I'll have to confess, handled the situation with sheer genius. If I said it once, I bet I said it 4,000 times, "Why can't she be like the other two girls? Why can't she be like Susan and Julie? Just one day, just one day, if that youngin' would go all day long without griping and crying and whining, it'd be a red-letter day in my life." And, of course, kids do want to cooperate. She became a griper and a whiner and a complainer, exactly as she was being instructed to do.

Now, at that time, her nickname, if you can believe this for a cute little girl with her two front teeth missing, was "Tadpole." I got involved in a study about what we're discussing right now and we made some changes. Every time somebody would come to visit, I'd always call her over to me and say, "Come here, baby." And I would say to the visitor, "I want to introduce you to the happiest, the sweetest, the friendliest little girl you have ever seen in your life. She's always laughing and talking and playing and just having a good time, aren't you, baby?"

"Yes, sir."

"Tell them what your name is, baby."

She said, "It's Tadpole."

This became a routine and it went on for about a month when one day when I said, "Tell them what your name is, baby."

She said, "Uh-uh, Daddy. I've changed my name."

"Oh, what's your name now, baby?"

She said, "I'm the Happy Tadpole."

In one month's time, in one month's time, it happened. She responded to the treatment and the words that were spoken over her.

To build good relationships, we must look for the good, be noncritical, and nonjudgmental.

When you change the input, you change the output.

Now, that sounds enormously *simple* and it is, but that does not necessarily mean it is *easy* because children and employees and peers and associates and other family members often are very, very trying. But to build good relationships, we must learn the discipline of looking for the good, of being noncritical and nonjudgmental; we must understand that when we throw dirt, saying ugly things about other people, we're not doing anything good in the world; in fact we're losing ground. When we understand that, we get ahead.

When we remember that a dog got to be our best friend by wagging his tail and not his tongue, then we've taken another step toward winning friends and influencing a lot of people.

A HIGH-QUALITY LIFE

I'd like to share with you a story of one of the most remarkable people I have ever had the privilege of knowing. She was a tremendous people expert. She was enormously successful. Not only did she have a very high standard of living, but she had an incredibly high quality of life. There's a vast difference between the two in many instances.

This lady, in December 1957, under rather difficult circumstances, started her company. She had really no choice because the company she had been working for had just fired her the day before. She had been there many years and had been largely responsible for the growth of that particular company. But she had a real dispute with management over some of the policies, and she had protested so vehemently that they decided enough was enough—and she was gone.

When she awakened the next morning, her desk had been comfortably placed right there on her front porch. She was absolutely devastated and she remained devastated for all of two or three minutes before she got her wits back together and decided that she was going to do something about it. She started her own company.

She immediately had an enormously successful business. As a matter of fact, she grew so fast that she had to seek a loan from the bank. She went to the bank for a $6,000 loan, and the first bank turned her down, and the second bank turned her down. They had lots of reasons for turning her down. First of all, it was a brand-new business. Second, she was a woman, and as you know, at that period of time women just didn't do things like go out and start their own companies.

Third, she had no experience as far as running a business was concerned. Fourth, she was going to build a business on Christian principles. She was going to pay her bills, as she always had, when they became due. She honestly believed that customer and salesperson and the company could always, all three of them, win in every single transaction. She opened every meeting with prayer. There were a lot of weird things that this lady believed in doing.

Her son, Don Carter, also believed in hiring handicapped people, that not only was it the proper thing to do, but they were very productive, which is a profitable approach to business. She built her business on faith, integrity, hard work, and opportunity for all. She coined a lot of phrases around what she built her business, but is so wrapped up in love and concern for others and the total concept that if you properly treat other people, the results have got to be good.

"Develop a swelled heart, not a swelled head."

Some of the favorite phrases of hers that I like the most are, "Don't get the rabbit habit. Think mink." Now, that's a beautiful phrase. And this is a prime one: "People need loving the most when they deserve it the least." Isn't that true? "Worry is a misuse of the imagination." "Don't be an *if* thinker, be a *how* thinker." "Develop a swelled heart, not a swelled head."

And if anybody ever had a swelled heart, it was Mary Crowley. She gave away literally tens of millions of dollars to very worthy causes. There are thousands of young men and women in our country today who have a college education because of her generosity.

One of her other favorites of mine: "You may give out but never give up." She built a business that does in excess of a half-billion dollar a year—Home Interiors and Gifts. Though she has gone to her enteral reward, her business is an example that any attorney in the world could take into a court of law and prove beyond any doubt that you can have everything in life you want, if you help enough other people get what they want.

I used to say that I thought Mary C. Crowley was the smartest businesswoman I'd ever met. I changed that the last few years of her life as I came to know her better. I didn't just think it; she really was the smartest business-person I ever met, an incredible human being.

She was a classic example that proves Leo Durocher was wrong when he said that, "Good guys finish last." Of course, we know that statement was wrong when he made it because there are many good people who have proved it wrong. I think the 1988 Super Bowl is another classic example of what I'm talking about—when Dan Reeves, the coach of the Denver Broncos, and Joe Gibbs, the coach of the Washington Redskins, met in the Super Bowl. You will never find two finer good guys than Dan Reeves and Joe Gibbs. Outstanding examples of what leadership is all about.

Another tremendous example is the former coach at UCLA, Coach John Wooden. John Wooden had some unique philosophies. For example, he was just as con-cerned with the morals of his players as he was with their quickness. Incredibly enough, this man, whose team won ten of twelve National Championships including seven in a row, the winningest coach of all from a percentage point of view and a National Championship point of view, this man never talked to his team about winning. He said, "Wins will take care of themselves. When you give your best effort, that is what makes you a winner."

I have said it, I guess, 10,000 times. I'm not talking about you beating somebody else; I'm talking about you becoming number one. I fervently believe, as did John Wooden, that when you get up in the morning and look in the mirror and say, "Today, I'm going to do my very best," and if at the end of the day, you can look right in the mirror and again say, "Today, I did my very best," I believe you are number one as far as the most important person in the world is concerned—and that is you.

When you give your best effort, that is what makes you a winner.

Best effort is all that is required, not only to have an acceptable standard of living, but more importantly, an even more acceptable quality of life.

COMPASSION

I love the story that is told about Vince Lombardi. He was the coach of the Green Bay Packers, the one who was so highly respected as the man who really kind of revolutionized football. He took a losing situation in Green Bay and built it into a championship team. They won the first two Super Bowls; they won the two championships before that.

One day in practice, a big guard was simply dogging it. Lombardi, as only Lombardi could do, pulled him out and he raked him over the coals from one end to the other. He said, "You're a lousy football player. You're not blocking, you're not tackling, you're playing a lousy game of football. Go to the dressing room." Well, the football player went to the dressing room absolutely broken-hearted. He had been their number-one draft choice and as far as he could then tell at that moment, it was all over.

An hour later when Lombardi brought the rest of the Packers into the locker room after the practice was over, he noticed that his young guard was still seated there on the bench. His head was in his hands and it was obvious that he had been doing some crying. As a matter of fact, was still sobbing.

Lombardi—ever the compassionate, often the change-able, always the leader that made him the winner—walked over and put his hand on the young guard's shoulder. He said, "Son, I did tell you the truth. You are a lousy football player. You're not blocking, you're not tackling, you're not putting out. But," he said, "I should have finished the story...because inside of you, son, there is an incredibly talented, productive player, and I'm going to be right by your side working with you until that talented football player inside of you comes out and asserts himself on the field."

With that, Jerry Kramer stood up. He felt much better, so much better that he went on to become the number-one pulling guard in the first fifty years of professional football.

I wonder how many outstanding people are right there inside of those we deal with every day. It's so easy to find fault and some people find fault like there was a reward for it—but it is so much *more important* and so much *more exciting* and so much *more beneficial* to look for the good.

It is so much more important, more exciting, and more beneficial to look for the good in people.

When Coach Lombardi left Green Bay for retirement, after one year, he was very unhappy in retirement, so he moved down to Washington to coach the team there. They had a quarterback who was very talented, but he was one of those free spirits. His name was Sonny Jurgenson. Much of the media wondered how Lombardi, the stern disciplinarian, was going to handle this free spirit who had a mind of his own. But the issue was settled on the first day of practice.

Several members of the media asked the question directly. "Coach, how are you going to handle Sonny Jurgenson?" Lombardi called Jurgenson over to him and he said to the members of the press, "Gentlemen, I would like to introduce you to the greatest quarterback who ever stepped on a football field. This is our quarterback, Sonny Jurgenson." Is it any wonder that he had the best year in his entire football career?

JUDGING OURSELVES AND OTHERS

In building relationships and establishing relationships and in our everyday life, too many of us have what we call double standards. We judge ourselves by one standard and we judge others by an entirely different standard.

A baker, for example, took a farmer into court. The farmer had been selling him his butter over a period of time and he discovered that one pound of butter only weighed fifteen ounces, and this had been going on for some little while. So they both stood before the judge and the judge said to the farmer, "Do you have an explanation for this?"

The farmer said, "Well, yes, I do." He said, "I lost my one-pound weight. But I have a pair of balance scales so I have been taking a loaf of bread from the baker and I've been using that as the balance."

Be careful when judging.

Isn't that ironic when you think about it? The reality of that story goes a little deeper than perhaps meets the eye. Not only should we be careful about how we judge, but it emphasizes that you really can't cheat anybody else.

The farmer was not obviously cheating on purpose. I doubt that the baker was cheating on purpose or he certainly would not have had him in court. But a lot of times—when we're so sure that somebody else is a crook and a scoundrel and a no-good—it encourages us to investigate a little more carefully, take a little more time to think about the matter. Get on his or her side of the table. Look at the issue from their perspective.

Many of our problems could be solved if we learned to evaluate others in exactly the same way we evaluate ourselves. Let me share these thoughts about judgments with you:

- When the other person blows up, he's nasty. When you do it, it's righteous indignation.

- When she's set in her ways, she's obstinate. When you are, you're just being firm.

- When he doesn't like your friends, he's prejudiced. When you don't like them, you're

155

simply showing good judgment of human nature.

- When she tries to be accommodating, she's polishing the apple. When you do it, you're using tact.

- When he takes time to do things, he's lazy. When you take ages, you're deliberate.

- When she picks flaws, she's picky. When you do, you're discriminating.

- When he reads the riot act, he's vicious and insensitive. When you do it, you're just being honest for their own good.

Isn't it amazing how we set those double standards? Rare indeed is the person who can weigh the faults of others without putting his or her thumb on the scale.

THE MOST IMPORTANT WORDS

Successful leaders and managers and people with lots of friends use several key phrases as needed when they're wrong—and is there anybody who's never made a mistake? When they're wrong, they say, *"I'm sorry. I made a mistake."* The six most important words in the language.

For whatever reason, parents think, at the ripe old age of thirty or thirty-five, *What does that eight or ten-year-old kid know about life? I don't need to explain.* It's difficult sometimes for parents to acknowledge that they were wrong and that they made a mistake. But I'm telling you, when mistakes happen, I don't care if the parent or grandparent is sixty-five years old and the child is five, those words can make a dramatic difference to the child and to the adult.

- The five most important words, *"You did a good job."*

- The four most important words, *"What is your opinion?"* and one of the great friend-makers of all time.

- Three most important words, *"Would you please?"*

- Two most important words are *"Thank you."*

- Most important word is *"You"*

- The least important word is *"Me."*

It's absolutely true that humankind does not live by bread alone; from time to time, we need buttering up a little bit. No truer words.

I love this following story and I think it epitomizes much of what I am talking about. This is the story of Benjamin Disraeli and William Gladstone, two of the great prime ministers in the British Empire of the last century—and political opponents.

A lady had the privilege of being seated next to Mr. Gladstone one evening at an affair of state. Those type of dinners went on for hours; and by and large, the people generally talked to the person next to them. At the end of the evening, and it had been a magnificent evening, the lady realized that she was going to be invited later on to attend a session with Mr. Disraeli. It seems that Gladstone was going out, Disraeli was coming in, or vice versa, and she would be seated next to both of them, separately, that evening. She spent several hours with each discussing and talking.

When the evening came to a close, somebody asked the lady to give her opinion of the two men, Gladstone and Disraeli. She said, "You know, when I spent the evening with Mr. Gladstone, I was absolutely convinced that here was one of the most charming men I'd ever met, one of the brightest, one of the best-informed human beings on the face of this earth. I was convinced he was an absolute genius. When I spent the evening with Mr. Disraeli, I was convinced that *I* was one of the nicest people, that I was one of the brightest people, that I was one of the best-informed people, that I was one of the friendliest people anywhere."

A key in winning relationships is to let the other person feel important.

It doesn't take anything else to understand why Mr. Disraeli was her favorite, does it? *The way you see people is the way you treat them.* A key in winning relationships is to let the other person feel important. Put them in a position where they are important because all people are basically important. It's amazing how we can learn from those who apparently have nothing to teach, but there is one person who is smarter than anyone, and that's everyone. If we can remember that, who knows where that really great idea is going to come from?

LISTEN AND LEARN—FROM EVERYONE

I think you may have heard the following story, but it bears repeating at this point.

A big tractor trailer got stuck underneath an overpass. They brought in the engineers and the experts who were trying to figure out a way to get this big thing on through. I mean, it was really stuck. They estimated that it would take hours and hours and cost thousands and thousands of dollars to dismantle part of the bridge or part of the truck. A little boy about ten years old gave them the solution when he suggested they simply take a little air out of the tires and the truck could drive right on through.

I hope that's a true story. It is so good that it just *has* to be true. But the point is obviously the same: we can learn, if we are responsive and receptive and open, from just about anyone.

According to the experts, on everybody's chest there is a sign that simply says, *"Make me feel important."*

Not long after we moved to Dallas, I was speaking for an insurance company at one of the major hotels. I was seated up front with a couple of the vice presidents on this side, that makes a total of three of us, and there were three people on the other side. I was seated in the middle. We sat down and the waitress brought a salad, which is fairly standard in a banquet arrangement. I said, "Well, thank you." We chatted back and forth with the vice presidents. She came back with the coffee and poured us some and I said, "Well, thank you very much."

In a few minutes, she came back with the entrée and I said to her, "You know, I really appreciate this and I must commend you. It is amazing how effective and efficient you are in serving all of us, yet you never seem to be in any kind of a hurry, and you have such a good attitude about it all."

She said, "Well my goodness, thank you very much. That makes it all worthwhile."

Dessert time came and they were serving ice cream with some chocolate syrup on it. Scouts honor, this is precisely what happened. The gentleman on either side of me got a little scoop of ice cream about the size of a golf ball with chocolate syrup on it. I received one bigger than a baseball. It was bigger than my fist. Matter of fact, it was larger than the scoop. It was such a dramatic difference that both of people on either side of me said, "Well, Zig, you obviously know this lady."

I said, "Well, I don't know her name but I sure know lots about her."

They asked, "Oh, what do you know about her?"

I said, "I know she's a human being and I know that she just responded in the way people respond when they have been appreciated."

All I had done was say, "Thank you."

The saying that "You can have everything in life you want if you just help enough other people get what they want," at this point, might sound a little selfish. I obviously was not complimenting her because I expected to get a bigger scoop of ice cream, but she responded in the only way she could to say thank you.

I'm telling you—when you make people feel important, when you treat them as human beings, then you will be ahead of the game. I don't care what the situation is or who the people are—it's true.

CHAPTER 10

Potential and Performance

I love this following story about the obscure college professor who had a wife whom he loved very much. His wife was hard of hearing. He went to work in his laboratories to develop a hearing aid so that he could communicate more easily and more effectively with his wife.

History tells us that he never did invent a hearing aid, but other than that, history has been unusually kind to Alexander Graham Bell because while he was working on the hearing aid doing a humanitarian thing because he loved his wife, he discovered the telephone procedures and techniques.

A little-known fact is that several years earlier, in 1861, a German inventor named Johann Reis had actually discovered a process for sending sound over the wires. And had he moved two of the electrodes one-one thousandth of an inch so that they touched, he would have been the inventor of the telephone, he would have been the one who discovered the method of sending voice over wire.

People who build winning relationships say and do things to and for others.

Now, I have no idea what Reis's motivation was or what his motives were, but I do know what the motivation of Alexander Graham Bell was, and it's just another way of saying that the good guys and gals are other-people oriented. They really are, by the concept of being good-finders. People who build winning relationships say and do things to and for others.

Now, I'm going to make a profound statement. I always tell my audiences when I'm about to make profound statements. I do that because an incredibly high percentage of my audiences do not recognize my profound statements as being profound if I don't tell them in advance—and I just don't want you to miss this. I'm not the one who said it.

Gossip can destroy you. Use a negative word on someone else and you feel some influence of that poison yourself. Make it a habit, use it on lots and lots of people, and all of that poison accumulates and it absolutely can be devastating. It's more than just a cliché that the best thing to do behind a man's back is to pat it, and easily the best way to remove a chip from somebody else's shoulder is to let him take a bow. Remember that you treat people like you see them, and those people who look down on others are generally living on a bluff.

Oh, when we think about those statements, how true they are.

REALIZING POTENTIAL THROUGH PERFORMANCE

I'll never forget one eye-opening experience that I had a number of years ago. A friend of mine, David Smith, invited me to be a substitute MC at the Elks Club Charity Ball. He said, "Zig, I don't know if you've ever been to an Elks Club dance and banquet, but," he said, "it's quite an occasion. I've invited a politician to be there, but you know how some of these politicians are." He said, "I'd like you to be there as the backup MC."

Well, I'd always wanted to be a backup MC at an Elks Club Charity Ball, so I said, "Okay, Mr. Smith, we'll go. My wife and I will be there."

165

We got there that evening and we were eating with David and his wife. After dinner, they got up and started dancing. Before we got up to dance, we watched David and his wife for a few minutes. I was in absolute awe. I could not believe what I was seeing. He was sixty-six years old, and he was a ballroom dancer—one of the most graceful men I think I've ever seen dance. It was a magnificent experience. As a matter of fact, the redhead and I never really danced that evening. We preferred to watch them.

The first time he came back to the table, I said, "Mr. Smith, I'm in awe. I didn't know you could dance like that."

He was somewhat embarrassed and said, "Well, to tell you the truth, for a number of years, I've been teaching ballroom dancing."

The David Smith I'm talking about was our yardman. One of the hardest-working men I've ever seen in my life. At age seventeen, he had to drop out of high school to support his family. At age twenty-two, he went back to school and got his diploma from high school at age twenty-five. He put his daughters through college because of his work ethic. He started as a yardman, and then he got into landscaping and other jobs.

The message, the eye-opener that I'm trying to communicate is that we should never judge a book by its cover. We should not. Mr. Smith was our yardman for about three years. I'm embarrassed to say I knew absolutely nothing about him until that night, except that he was a hard worker who did an excellent job. On hot August days, he would get out there and work at a steady pace. It would've killed me, I guarantee you, in thirty minutes to follow him around. But he had taken that station in life at the time, the only job he could get. But he didn't stop at just cutting the grass and doing the edging; he studied and learned how to be a landscaper and, as a result, made a beautiful living because of it.

One of the most fascinating aspects about this concept of potential and performance was told to me one morning by a lady you may have heard of—Mary Kay Ash. I was speaking to a group and toward the end of the talk, she walked in and sat there listening for a few minutes. When it was over, she invited me to come in and talk with her about some future activity.

She started telling me about her start in business. During the Depression, she was a Stanley dealer. She was a widow with small children and living in Houston. She was selling Stanley brushes, and she had been averaging $7 a party in sales, and the gift she gave to the hostess cost her $5. Not exactly a money-making endeavor.

Then she heard about the Stanley National Convention to be held in Dallas, Texas. She borrowed the $12 necessary for the transportation and the three nights in the hotel for the convention. Remember, this was during the Depression years, 1929-1939. Mary Kay's friends thought she was absolutely crazy to waste that $12 because what she needed to do was really look for a job so she could support her family, but she was determined to attend.

During the three days, Mary Kay camped on the doorstep of everyone who was extremely productive. When mealtime came around, the $12 did not include the meals, so she always made an excuse and went to her room. There she ate cheese and crackers for three days; that's what she brought along to eat.

On the night of the final banquet, when they honored the queen of sales, Mary Kay said there was a gorgeous brunette, tall and striking, whom she had been talking with all week, whom she had asked hundreds of questions, whom she had persuaded to put on a mock party so she could watch how she was doing it because she was the best in the country. That night, during the banquet awards, Mr. Stanley Beveridge, the president of the company, was there. Every lady would walk down the aisle and Mr. Beveridge would shake hands with them.

Mary Kay said she was somewhere about in the middle of the pack when she walked up to him. She told me, "I'm certain there are a lot of people who said exactly the same thing I was going to say, but I stood in front of him that night and said, 'Mr. Beveridge, you don't know who I am tonight, but next year at this time you will, because I'm going to be the queen of sales.'"

He could have said, "Sure, young lady. Sure, I know you are." He'd probably been told that by twenty ladies before Mary Kay reached him. He could have sloughed her off as being enthusiastic and making a big promise then disappearing forever. But Mary Kay said the most meaningful moment of her career took place right there when Mr. Beveridge quietly, calmly, and deliberately looked her right in the eye. She told me, "For what seemed like forever, he said nothing. And then he said, 'You know, young lady, somehow or other, I believe you will.'" Mary Kay said that his comment had a profound impact on her life. The next year, she was the queen of sales.

Treat people around you in terms of potential rather than just performance.

A lot of people have gone a lot farther in life than they thought they could because somebody else thought they could. We need to be encouragers. Gordon McDonald says it well: "My wife, Gail, and I try to treat the people around us in terms of potential rather than just performance." When you think about it, that outlook makes an awful lot of sense. *Sometimes one act, one simple act, can affect literally millions and millions of people.*

ONE SIMPLE ACT

For example, many years ago, just outside of Boston, there was a mental institution that was way ahead of its time. They had gained a substantial reputation for their ability to deal with and help people who had mental problems; but even in that enlightened institution, they had a dungeon. In the dungeon, they would put the hopelessly insane, those for whom nothing could be done at the time.

A little girl was there. She was known simply as Little Annie. One day Little Annie was just as sane and reasonable as anybody; but the next day, she would be vicious and attack almost anybody who came within range.

There was an elderly nurse who worked at the hospital, and she was getting ready for retirement. As a matter of habit each day, she started going down to the dungeon at lunchtime and sitting next to the cage where Little Annie was kept. Sometimes she would carry on a little conversation, sometimes she would say nothing; but always, she was there. One day, the nurse took some brownies along, and as she got ready to leave, she put the brownies on a little tray inside of Little Annie's cage. When she went back the next day, the brownies were gone. So once each week thereafter, she left brownies for the little girl.

A few weeks later, the doctors noticed that Little Annie was making remarkable progress. They decided maybe something could be done. They moved her upstairs. Over a period of years, her emotional stability, her mental health, was completely restored and they came to her one day, and they said, "Little Annie, you may go home if you would like."

She said, "No, this place has meant so much to me. I would like to stay here a few years longer and I would like to be able to make a contribution to some others as my way of saying thank you to this institution for what it has done for me."

Many, many years later, when Queen Victoria of England was pinning England's highest award on Helen Keller, Queen Victoria asked, "Helen, to whom or to what do you owe your remarkable progress, your remarkable accomplishments in life, the fact that you've favorably influenced and had an impact on literally millions and millions of lives?"

Helen Keller said, "Had it not been for Anne Sullivan, Little Annie, nobody would have ever known who Helen Keller was."

You never know, when you throw the pebble in the stream or the lake, how far the circles are going to go. Likewise, you never know how far your words of encouragement will go to make a beautiful circle surrounding many people's lives. *The way you treat people can make a dramatic difference in the way they handle life.*

A PURPOSE AND REASON

Right here in Italy, Texas, there was a little girl named Linda Isaacs. Linda is a black girl, born with dwarfism, and was diagnosed when she was about four years old as being learning disabled. But when she was six years old, they put her in the first grade. Her mother and family said to the teachers, "Now don't worry about trying to teach Linda anything, she can't learn, but she's a pleasant little girl. Her classmates will adopt her, make her the class mascot, she'll be called Shorty, but she'll be very popular and everybody will just love her."

Well, that's exactly what happened. They didn't try to teach her anything so she didn't learn anything. At the end of the first year, they decided that instead of holding her back, they would move her on up to the second grade, because otherwise she's not going to learn anything in either grade and they didn't want her to make a new set of friends every year.

Linda Isaacs graduated from high school functioning at the first-grade level. Now, you tell me, what were her chances in life? I think you'd agree they were very, very slim indeed.

But Linda Isaacs' mother was getting on up in years, so she brought Linda to Dallas to live with an older sister. The older sister took her to Goodwill Industries where she met a lady named Carol Klep. Carol took one look at Linda Isaacs and she did not see a helpless, hopeless little

172

girl who would be a ward of the state all of her life. She saw a little girl who was obviously put here for a purpose. There was a reason for her being here and she determined she was going to find out what that reason was.

They gave Linda some more evaluations and discovered that she could indeed learn some things. They gave her a simple job, which she actually outgrew that afternoon. The next day, they gave her two more jobs that she quickly outgrew.

Now go forward with me twelve months—and twelve months later, Linda Isaacs was answering the telephone, checking the payroll, and functioning almost as a full-fledged secretary. She learned more in twelve months than she had in eighteen years. For eighteen years, Linda Isaacs had been repeatedly told, "Linda can't learn, Linda can't learn, Linda can't learn," and for eighteen years, Linda Isaacs had been repeating it back to herself: "Linda can't learn, Linda can't learn, Linda can't learn." It's absolutely true that as you sow, so also shall you reap.

The computer people are right—garbage in, garbage out. We're right when we say you put the good stuff in, you get the good stuff out. All of a sudden, the input changes. Somebody says, "Linda can learn, Linda can learn, Linda can learn," and Linda Isaacs, in wild-eyed astonishment then started saying, "Linda can learn."

Now please don't misunderstand. I'm not saying that all you have to do is say "I can" and everything is wonderful. But I am saying this: I cannot help but wonder how many people have been consigned to a life of mediocrity because they were repeatedly told, "You can't, you can't, you can't."

As mentioned in Chapter 2, Shad Helmstetter states in his book *What to Say When You Talk to Your Self* that the average eighteen-year-old American has been told 148,000 times, "No," or, "You can't do it." When we tell youngsters 148,000 times they can't do something, I can guarantee you, they'll believe it.

The greatest good we can do for others is not just to share our riches with them, but to reveal theirs to them. Others express it this way: When you give a man a fish, you feed him for the day; teach him to fish, and you feed him for life.

Again, don't misunderstand. I'm not saying that all you have do is say, "You can do it," and the other person will be able to do it. The question often comes up, or I might emphasize over on top of that by saying, "They've got an infinitely better chance of doing it if you tell them they can instead of telling them they can't." To be fair, I believe we should give them the benefit of the doubt.

DISCOURAGE MEDIOCRITY

A lot of times people have either thought it or they've said to me, "Now wait a minute Ziglar, suppose my child does a lousy job. Suppose she drops the ball. Suppose he fouls up. Suppose my employees don't do the job they're supposed to. Am I still supposed to brag on them?" No.

I think that's the worst thing you could possibly do. That encourages mediocrity.

A minority race person in San Francisco brought suit against the school system because the entire time the student was attending school, the person was told over and over, "You're doing good. You're doing good. You're doing good." And then when the person graduated, the reality was that the graduate could not get a job because the person had not received an education.

I believe that my mother has the correct answer. When I was a child in Yazoo City, Mississippi, since dad had died we all had to go to work at a young age. By the time I was eight years old, I was milking a cow and working in the garden. I told a story about cows in Chapter 8. You may be a city slicker and don't know much about cows, so let me just tell you one little thing about cows. Cows don't *give* milk. I'm here to tell you, you gotta fight for every drop of it.

She expected that we do our very best.

I'll never forget that first solo assignment I had in the garden. There were certain things we knew about our mother. We knew what she expected when she gave us an assignment—she expected that we do our very best. We also knew that she was going to inspect to make certain she got what she expected. We also knew that she was going to teach us how to do what she expected us to do.

One of the most frustrating things parents and managers can do to their children or their employees is to tell them to do something and then not teach them or show them how to do it correctly. They need to know how to do that particular thing, why it is to be done, give them the reasons for doing it, and show them or teach them the ways to do it. Mother always taught us how and she told us why. And then if we did a good job, she would always compliment us—but she always inspected to make sure we did what she had expected us to do.

For this first solo assignment, I had to hoe two rows of beans and they were three and a half miles long. Would you believe three miles long? Well, when you're eight years old, it looked like they were three and a half miles long. Mother showed me exactly what she wanted me to do and then she said, "Son, when you get through, call me." Well, I finally finished. I called my mom. I said, "Momma, I'm through."

My momma was a little bitty lady, only about five feet tall, and she weighed less than 100 pounds. She was slightly stooped at that time. She always wore a little cloth sun bonnet on her head to protect her face from that hot Mississippi sun. When Momma was dissatisfied with something we had done, she would always fold her hands behind her back, she would always duck her head, she would always cock it slightly to the right, and she would always give that little left to right motion that said, "Uh-uh." My momma looked at my work and then started that left to right nod; I said, "What's the matter, Momma?" Momma smiled a little bit and she said, "Well, son, it looks like you're going to have to lick this calf over."

She criticized the performance but she praised the performer.

Now, is there anybody who does not understand that perfectly, immensely clear old colloquial Mississippi term, "Lick the calf over"? Well, what that means in a nutshell is, "Son, this is unsatisfactory. You're going to have to do the job over." I knew perfectly good and well what my momma was telling me, but I was just trying to buy time. So I looked at her, I kind of grinned, I said, "Momma, I haven't been messing with the calf. I've been hoeing these beans." Momma kind of laughs and says, "Well, son, what I mean is this: for most boys, what you've done would have been perfectly all right, but you're not most boys. You're my son, and my son can do better than this."

You see, she had criticized the performance. It needed to be criticized. But she had praised the performer because he needed the praise. I started working on those rows of beans again with my self-image completely intact.

I believe that's the best procedure in building winning relationships with other people. When we have to deal with a productivity factor that is unsatisfactory, a performance that is not up to standards, I believe we need to remember that we do not chastise or criticize the individual, but we deal rather with the performance of that individual. I believe that's the way to build more winning relationships. Help that person to be more productive, help that individual to have a higher self-esteem, and overall it will be best for everyone concerned.

I close this chapter with the following story.

Many years ago in Europe, an old man sat in a cathedral playing the organ. He was a skilled musician. The old cathedral was absolutely beautiful; and as the sun was setting you could see the sun coming through the stained-glass windows. Watching the old musician playing, he took on an absolutely angelic appearance. He filled that church with beautiful, beautiful music; yet it was sad and melancholy because today was his last day. He was being replaced by a younger organist.

At dusk, the back door of the cathedral opened up rather brusquely and a young man stepped inside. The old organist looked at him and recognized who he was. He reached up and removed the key, put it in his pocket, and headed for the back door. When he drew abreast of the young man, the young man just held out his hands and with a few simple words said, "Please, the key." The old man put the key in the hand of the young organist. The young organist almost literally ran to the organ and he looked at the bench and he looked at the organ for just a moment, then he sat down, inserted the key, turned it on, and started to play.

While the old man had played beautifully and skillfully, the young man played with sheer genius. Music filled the cathedral, it filled the town, it filled the countryside, music such as they had never heard around there.

This was the world's introduction to the music of Johann Sebastian Bach. With tears streaming down his cheeks, the old man said, "Suppose, just suppose, I had not given the master the key."

I believe inside of every human being, that's you included, there is incredible ability and intelligence. I believe the best way to get our own talent out is to start looking for the talent in others, encouraging them— because it is absolutely true that you can have everything in life you want if you help enough other people get what they want.

CHAPTER 11

A Most Fortunate Life

Over a period of years, many people have asked me to speak after they have read one of my books, watched one of the videos, or they heard one of the audio cassettes. They form a mental picture of exactly who old Zig is and what he looks like, and most people are generally surprised when they meet me to discover that I'm so young and handsome and vibrant and enthusiastic. They thought I was some old codger, a fifty- or sixty-year-old standing up there doing all of that talking.

On the serious side, a lot of people do form some interesting pictures of who I am, where I came from, what I've been doing. Let me share with you that I am indeed a most fortunate man. I've traveled more than three million miles all around the globe. I have friends, acquaintances, and associates in high places. I've seen the valleys, the mountains, and the ocean all at the same time, while I was trying to hit a seven iron to the green on the island of Maui. Beautiful, beautiful sight. I've flown in the Concord at 60,000 feet. At 60,000 feet doing more than twice the speed of sound, I could literally see the curvature of the earth underneath me.

I don't know what you can do with this next bit of information, but maybe we can find some use for it somewhere. The Concord literally stretches about eighteen inches while it is in flight. The metal stretches. Fascinating. Maybe we can apply it this way. Maybe when we're flying our highest, which is the purpose of this book, *You're a Natural Champion,* maybe that means that we are stretching and using resources that we've never used before.

I've seen a rhino on safari who was grievously wounded in a battle for a mate. I've seen the deceptively dangerous hippo. A lot of people don't know it, but the hippo kills more people every year than any other wild game animal in all of Africa. I've seen a pride of lions from about fifty feet away. My son and I climbed to the top of Cape Point in South Africa and we had a chance to watch the green of the Indian Ocean come together with the blue of the Atlantic Ocean in what has got to be one of the most beautiful sights on the face of this earth.

On October 5, 1985, I realized a lifetime dream. I moved into a beautiful home overlooking the fifteenth tee on the Queens golf course at Gleneagles, which is a very fine country club. I drive a nice car. I wear nice clothes. I have a high standard of living. More importantly though, I have a good quality of life.

I have a high standard of living. More importantly though, I have a good quality of life.

The reason I mention all of this along with a wife of forty-one years, who vows that she really does love me, and have four beautiful children whom I obviously love. I also have three sons-in-love and one daughter-in-love. We believe daughter- and sons-in-*law* is a little too harsh for these particular people because they are such loving, gentle people.

Even more importantly, I have a right relationship with my heavenly Father. He's given me a written guarantee that I will spend eternity with Him. Yes, life has been very, very good to me.

But things haven't always been that way and what you're seeing is not what started out. What you're reading and the person who said it is dramatically different from the one who grew up in Yazoo City, Mississippi.

I want to share my story with you because I believe that my story really is your story. I believe that with three exceptions, I have walked in every single pair of shoes who will ever read this book.

The three exceptions are these:

1) I've never lost a mate or a child through death or divorce. If you've had those traumatic experiences, I might look at you and say, "I know how you feel," but the reality is no one else can know how you feel because they don't know the depth of your affection and commitment to the one who is no longer with you, whether it be from death or divorce. I cannot say I've walked in your shoes.

2) All of my life, I've enjoyed marvelous physical and emotional health. If you've had any health problems in your life, I mean serious health problems, I can look at you and say, "Well, I know how you feel," but the truth is I really do not know how you feel because I've always had good health.

3) I've always had somebody who loved me. If you have not had that, I can say to you, "I know how you feel," and I can try and I really do try, but the reality is I cannot truthfully imagine how you do feel.

As a child, though I was from a large family, I was deeply loved by my mother. She always had time for each one of us individually. My wife and I have had a wonderful relationship. I have a marvelous relationship with each of my children and each of my three sons-in-love and my daughter-in-love. My children and I get along extraordinarily well. We have a marvelous, marvelous relationship.

But as far as being despondent, friend, I've been there. As far as being down in the dumps, I have been there. As far as being broke, I don't believe there's anybody who will ever listen to this particular presentation who's ever been any broker than I have been. As far as having any lack of direction, I don't believe anybody was ever as confused, not about just where they were going to be a year from now and five years from now, but I'm talking about being confused about what you would be doing tomorrow. I too have walked in that pair of shoes, if you have had those experiences.

HOPE AND ENCOURAGEMENT

I share my story because I believe it's a story that will give you some hope and some encouragement. When I was five years old, my dad died. I'm one of twelve children; I was the tenth of twelve. Dad died on Thursday; my baby sister died the following Tuesday. It was in the heart of the Depression years, the toughest Depression this country has ever seen. There were six of us who were too young to work. We survived because our mother had

185

such incredible faith, was such a hard worker, had more common sense than just about anybody I have ever seen. We survived because we had those five milk cows and because we had that big garden and we derived a great deal of our foodstuffs and means of making a living right from that.

"When a task is once begun, you leave it not until it's done; and be it matter great or small, you do it well or not at all."

I had a mother who also had incredible wisdom. She just had something about her that kind of set her apart. She only finished the fifth grade, but as a child she saturated us with those little "sonnet sermons," one of them I so well remember: "When a task is once begun, you leave it not until it's done; and be it matter great or small, you do it well or not at all."

When her grandchildren from my marriage started making their appearance, she used to say to me over and over every time we'd get together, "Son, your children will pay more attention to what you do than what you say." Over and over she would say, "If you will set the example, you don't need to bother about setting the rules because they're going to do exactly what they see you doing."

What a fortunate man I have been. When I was in the first grade, Mrs. Dement Warren, my first-grade teacher, took an interest in me. Now that's extraordinarily important because when I was in the first grade there in Yazoo City, Mississippi, I had all of the childhood diseases. I had the mumps and the measles and the whooping cough. I had them all in first grade. I missed more than four months of attending school. Mrs. Warren, though, twice a week would come out to my house and she would spend an hour or two going over the lessons with me, teaching what I'd missed in class and giving me the assignments that I needed to catch up.

Had she not done that, I would have failed the first grade. Had I failed the first grade, I would have been drafted into the military out of high school and a college education would have been completely out of my reach when the war was over. Almost everything hinged on me getting out of the first grade on time. Obviously I did not know that at the time, and I can't tell you that I was very enthused about Mrs. Warren coming to our home twice a week and spending all of that time with me, but how fortunate I am. I'm so fortunate because she taught me how to read, and in the sixth grade Mrs. Whirley taught me to love to read.

LESSONS IN AND OUT OF THE CLASSROOM

I went to work in a grocery store before I was ten years old. I was a teller in the grocery store. I'm not trying to impress you with the title; that just meant that I told people to move while I swept. I was not the manager, is what I'm saying. Mr. John R. Anderson was the owner of the store and he had a large plantation about ten miles out of town. He became almost a father to me. He and his wife did not have any children.

One afternoon a week he used to take me out to the farm and let me ride around and see everything and watch him talk with the people there who were doing the farming. He taught me about free enterprise. I will remember that hot, hot summer day.

In those years, about 90 percent of the business, literally, was done from noon on Friday until midnight on Saturday. That's when the farmers came in town to buy their groceries, that's when the town people got paid and they had some money to buy the groceries. I well remember that day there in the grocery store when nothing was going on, I mean nothing.

Mr. Anderson was somewhat careful with his money, meaning that he liked to get about $1.50 worth of value out of every dollar; and when he saw all of us just standing around, he said to me, "Boy, can't you do something? Look at those shelves, they're all messed up. Why look at that right there. Straighten it up. Do something with it."

I looked at him and said, "Mr. Anderson, it's just two cans of tomatoes." I guess it was the *way* I said it that really got to him because he reached over and grabbed me by the shoulder and said, "Let me tell you something, boy. That case of tomatoes had twenty-four cans in it to begin with. We've now sold the twenty-two cans, which means we have got our money back. Now as soon as we sell those two there will be profit. It's out of profit that I pay you your salary. Now," he said, "what do you think of those two cans of tomatoes?"

I said, "Mr. Anderson, they're absolutely beautiful." For the first time I understood that I was involved.

As a youngster, we lived in a big old house; rent was $10 a month. That's back when $10 was a whole lot of money. There were seven steps leading up to the front porch. On hot summer nights, a couple of buddies of mine, Red Wallace and Lou Russell Williams, would come over and we'd play together. We frequently ended up on that top step fighting the Ford versus Chevrolet war.

Mr. Fred Shirley, the rural mail carrier who lived down the street, drove a Chevrolet and every year he would go down and trade in that little Chevrolet coupe on a new one. As a child it was my dream that when I got to be a man that I'd be able to go down to the Chevrolet dealership, and when Mr. Shirley traded in his little coupe for a new one, I'd be able to buy that secondhand car. You could buy a new car in those days for $500, a secondhand one was only about $250 or $300.

In my childhood imagination, I was going to take that little car and every year when I got my vacation, which as everybody knows is two weeks, no more, no less, two weeks, I was going to get in that little coupe and drive it as far as it would go in one week and then I was going to turn it around and drive it back home the other week. It was clear in my mind.

Now Red Wallace and Lou Russell Williams were Ford guys. We used to fight those battles all the time. As a child, I believed and dreamed that one day when I got to be a man I was going to have me a whole acre of land on the outskirts of town. I never thought I would live in the slums. I was going to have an acre of ground, build a little house, and then when I got to the downside of life, when I had retired and my income was minimal and I needed something to supplement that income, I would have a big garden and I would raise and sell the vegetables to my neighbors to supplement my income. That was my dream as a child. It was the dream of a little guy from a little town who would struggle all of his life.

You cannot consistently perform in a manner that is inconsistent with the way you see yourself.

I want to emphasize something here and I'll emphasize it again before I get through. *The picture you have of yourself is exactly the way you will perform.* You cannot consistently perform in a manner that is inconsistent with the way you see yourself. You just can't.

As a youngster, I was very, very small. I weighed less than 120 pounds fully dressed when I was a senior in high school, and that was fully dressed. I was very aggressive when I was a youngster. If I'd get in an argument with somebody and we couldn't settle it in ten seconds or less, I would just rear back and I'd bust him—and I never discriminated. It made no difference to me whether the guy was tall or short or fat or slim or white or black or anything in between. If we couldn't settle it in ten seconds or less, I would just bust them one.

A Mexican boy completely broke me of that habit. But in my own defense, I will say I scared him half to death in the process, as there were a few seconds when he thought he'd killed me. That really did teach me quite a lesson.

One of the signs of an inferiority complex—which is what it was called in those days, today it's low self-esteem or poor self-image—is that the individual who cannot handle a situation will stomp their feet, slam the door, and run away. Well, during this time, children hit each other to settle matters and that's the way I dealt with situations. Otherwise, I was a good kid. I worked in the grocery store from the time I entered the fifth grade until the last year of high school. I also had a paper route that took me two nights a week to deliver, and one night a week to collect the cost from the people on that paper route. I was busy, very busy, as a child.

A CHANGE IN PLANS

I so well remember just before I was to go off and participate in World War II that I had the dream of being a naval aviator. And the night before I left, the man whom I'd gone to work for the year before, working with him in his meat market next door, was a man named Mr. Walton Hanning. Mr. Hanning was the same kind of man as Mr. Anderson. He became an advanced advisor for me. He taught me about commission selling; because when he would have a surplus of something, he'd always give me a little bonus if I helped to encourage people to buy that particular item on the last day of the week so we wouldn't have to carry it over the weekend.

The night before I was to report on July 1, 1944, Mr. Hanning said to me, "Zig, I would really like for you to come back after the war." We all knew it was about over. "When the war is over, I'd like you to come back and work for me."

I said, "Well, Mr. Hanning, I just wouldn't have any interest in that."

He said, "Why not?"

I said, "Well, there's just not any money in working in a meat market."

I was being paid $30 a week for that one last month before I went into the service. That was my full-time pay. When I say full time, I mean from 7:00 in the morning until 7:00 at night five days a week and from 7:00 in the morning until 11:30 at night on that sixth day.

He said, "Well, let me show you something, Zig. Last year after paying all of my taxes, I was still able to take home net $5,117 out of this market." That was his income for 1943, and in 1943 that represented an enormous sum of money in that little town. This is a place where the doctor, whom I loved and respected so much, had built a magnificent home and the price of it was a little over $4,000. So I'm talking about a lot of money when I say $5,117.

Mr. Hanning said, "Zig, if you would come back and work for me for two years, I will teach you everything you need to know about running a meat market, how to buy and how to sell. How to balance your books. I will help you establish a line of credit. I will help you get set up in your own business if you'll give me two years after you come back."

Wow was I was excited!

The next day when I left for the service, I just flew out of town. I was going to go off to that war, I was going to get that thing over with, I was going to come back, I was going to work a couple of years for Mr. Hanning, I was going to get my own meat market, and I was going to make me $5,117 in a single year. I was excited!

But on September 15, 1944, at six minutes after 9 o'clock, in the YWCA on State Street there in Jackson, Mississippi, when I walked in for the little party they were holding for us sailor boys, I saw standing over by the nickelodeon this gorgeous little redhead. Hair all the way to her shoulders. She had on a green pinafore dress, and I knew right then that life would never be the same again. Oh, I tell you, when I met that redhead, things changed and they changed rather dramatically. My plans changed.

When I was discharged, I decided to get my degree at the University of South Carolina. We were married and I was supporting the marriage by selling sandwiches along the dormitories at night. Business was exceptionally good during the winter months and the fall months. But during summer school, enrollment was way down and so my business went down to zero. The redhead saw an ad in the paper where they wanted a $10,000 a year salesman. We thought that was providential direction that they wanted a $10,000 salesman because we certainly wanted the $10,000. It seemed to be too much of a coincidence.

I went for the interview. I came home all excited and I told the redhead, I said, "Well, sweetheart, we got us a job. We're going to make $10,000 a year."

She said, "What are we going to be doing?"

I said, "It's in the cookware business," and incidentally I had to buy my own samples, it was on a reference or door-to-door selling some people call it. The informed call it the person-to-person approach to selling, strictly on commission, and I said, "Yeah, we'll be making all of that moncy."

She said, "When do we start?"

I said, "Well, I don't know exactly. The man said he would call." I was so naïve at that point in my life I thought I had the job when really I was just brushed off.

A month went by and I didn't hear from him and I started to question whether or not I was going to get that call. So I wrote him a letter, "I believe I can sell that product. It's a beautiful product. I need the job. I'm willing to work. Give me a chance." It took me another month to persuade him and then I had to accept the conditions, the arrangements he was willing to make. He said, "You take the training, which is one week. If at the end of the week, if at that point I think you can sell, then I will give you the opportunity."

I'm optimistic. I'm the kind
of fellow who'd put a dime in
the parking meter while his
wife goes shopping.

At that point I did not know what the rate of commission was and did not know whether or not I'd even get the job, but I was so convinced that during the week I'd persuade him to let me have the job that I took that training on faith and optimism that yes, I was going to be able to go to work. As you know by now, I'm optimistic. I'm the kind of fellow who'd put a dime in the parking meter while his wife goes shopping. That's my basic nature. It still took me another month to get the job.

DOWN BUT NOT OUT

Then for the next two and a half years all I did was prove they had been right to start with. Don't misunderstand. That doesn't mean I didn't sell a lot, because I did. I sold my furniture, I sold my car, and that's a little too close to the truth to be as funny to me as it is to you. I had literally gone down the grocery line, mis-figured the total, and had to put a loaf of bread back. That's when bread was a dime a loaf. I have literally had to make a sale so I could buy fifty cents' worth of gasoline so I could make my next sales call.

When my first baby was born, the hospital bill was $64. I didn't have $64. I had to go out and make two sales in order to get my own baby out of the hospital. They literally cut my lights off. They literally disconnected my telephone. In both cases, I got there just before they left and I was able to give them a check and get them to put my lights and my telephone back on.

I know what it is to be broke. I cannot tell you the number of nights I have gone to bed and I would say to myself, "Tomorrow I'm going to get out there and I'm going to knock them dead. I'm really going to do it." But it's one thing to do that in the comfort and security of your own bed. It's another thing to say it the next day when you have to go out and face the prospects, some of whom in my mind were very dangerous people. In my mind, my life was at stake on so many of those interviews.

As mentioned in Chapter 4, there have been many, many, many occasions when I would have a prospect right in front of me and another prospect right next door, and another prospect twenty miles down the highway and after failing to get in the first door, instead of going next door and knocking, I would drive twenty miles down the highway. In my mind I thought I needed the time to plan what I was going to say. I told myself that the reason I didn't get in the first house is because I didn't have a good plan. I justified it by saying, "At least I'm working."

A person with a poor self-image will do an awful lot of strange things.

A person with a poor self-image will do an awful lot of strange things. The sales manager who says they'll go to work as soon as they get broke enough does not understand that there is something that is considerably worse than being broke—and that is being rejected. Had I understood early in life what I learned many years later, my career would have been much easier. People don't really reject you personally. They refuse the business offer. They would have refused it from anyone who offered it to them. Once I learned that, it made a dramatic difference in my perspective.

CHAPTER 12

You <u>Are</u> a Natural Champion

I did some things as a young salesman that to this day I find difficult to believe, but I remember in vivid detail the day I'd been in the business eleven days. I had been knocking on doors every afternoon after finishing my classes. On this particular day, I had been knocking, I guess I had knocked on 200 doors. And I did not get invited in even once. Obviously everyone was not home.

I was on a daily drive in Columbia, South Carolina, two blocks before Devine Street, which was the major thoroughfare, and I said to myself, *If I don't at least get in one house to tell my story, this is it. I've had it. I've given it a fair chance. I'm going to quit.* When I knocked on the next to last door before Devine Street, a widow named Mrs. B.C. Deckert came to the door. I gave her the little story and she said, "Well, you know, the person you really ought to talk to is my sister-in-law, Mrs. J.O. Freeman next door." She has a real need for what you're selling.

So I literally ran next door. That had been the first ray of sunshine I had seen in a long time so I ran next door. I was so excited as I talked to Mrs. Freeman and she said, "Well, my husband would need to be here. Can you come by tonight?"

Well, it just happened that I could, so I went back that night. They were having dinner but they said, "Come on in and tell your story."

I said, "No, you go ahead and finish your dinner."

They got through and Mr. Freeman said, "My sister would like to see this too. Let me call her over." I made the presentation to all three of them and when I finished, Mr. Freeman said, "Well, I think I'll take a set."

It was set number 541. I vividly remember it. It cost 61 dollars and 45 cents. The down payment was 16 dollars and 45 cents. I wrote that order up, I got the check for $16.45 and I took a deep breath, scarcely believing my good fortune. I had finally made a sale. Oh boy, oh boy was I overexcited!

Finally, Mr. Freeman brought me back to earth and he said, "You know, Mr. Ziglar, I believe if you talk to

Mrs. Deckert, she might buy a set too." So with the air of a skilled professional salesman, I said to Mrs. Deckert, "Well, what about it, Mrs. Deckert?"

She said, "Well, I don't have any money with me."

And again, with all the tact and diplomacy of an experienced professional, I said, "Well shucks, you just live next door, go get your checkbook."

And interestingly enough, she said, "Okay."

She went next door, she got her checkbook, and I made the second sale.

The redhead and I lived upstairs at the time and I don't think I hit more than two steps on the way up. I was so excited about those two sales that we went out and bought two quarts of good ice cream. And we really, really had a celebration. And that is a literal truth.

I NEED HELP

I also remember a little later, things were so, so tough; we were struggling for survival. I persuaded my sales manager Bill Cranford, who by then was a good friend of mine, to go with me on a presentation. I said, "Bill, I have to make some sales. I'm doing something wrong. I need help." He went with me and at the end of the presentation we were back out in car and I said, "Well, Bill, what do you think?"

He said, "Zig, let me ask you, what are you selling?"

I said, "Now Bill, you know what I'm selling."

He said, "Yeah, I know, but don't you think you should have told the lady?"

I said, "Bill, it wasn't *that* bad."

He said, "Zig, I guarantee you that all the lady knows is the price. She has no idea what the set of cookware will do for her."

I said, "Bill, it just wasn't that bad."

He said, "Let's go to the training room." He had an old webcore wire recorder. We recorded my presentation. In a twenty-one-minute sales talk, I uhed 187 times by actual count. That is nine uh's per minute. It was "I, uh, well, uh, yeah uh, you see, uh." And I stress that because today is, you know, I'm known as the fastest "drawl" in the West.

That day, some of the guys were putting on group demonstrations. They would go into a home and cook a whole big meal and the hostess would invite several of her friends to see the demonstration. Their sales were two, three, and four times as much as mine because I wasn't doing group demonstrations. And so I wanted to do that.

But I had two basic problems. Number one, I didn't know how to cook and had never seen a demonstration. The second problem was I didn't have any money to buy the groceries or the premium set. But with a confidence that generally goes with ignorance, I figured that some-how or another I could deal with that.

I heard of Mrs. B.C. Moore who lived at 2210 High Street on the corner of High Street and Colonial Drive. She had a set of the cookware, but she didn't like it. She didn't know how to use it. So I decided I would go see Mrs. Moore with a plan. And I said, "Mrs. Moore, I want to teach you how to use that set of cookware if you'll buy the food to cook and invite in a couple of prospects."

She said, "You got yourself a deal." She invited Doctor and Mrs. Gay, he was a dentist, and they too had a set of the cookware and they didn't like it because they didn't know how to use it. She invited her sister and her husband who were living with them while their home was being built, Mr. and Mrs. Clarence Spence. And they invited Mr. and Mrs. M.P. Gates who lived down the street.

I'LL BUY!

I cooked the meal and apparently it was all right. At least I didn't burn anything. I finished serving the meal and talking to them about it. Then Mrs. Spence gave a five-minute speech on why they could not have or could not buy a set of the cookware. They're building a house. They've got all kinds of expenses, they're broke, they're in debt, and she raved on and on about why they couldn't buy a set. My heart was sinking lower and lower all the time. But she winded up by saying, "But we're always broke, were always in debt, and if I don't go ahead and get this set of cookware right now, I know we'll never have it." She said, "I'll take it."

Then Mrs. Gates made a five-minute speech about why they could not buy. She gave exactly the same reasons and then she wound up saying, "But we're always broke, we're always in debt, and if I don't get it now, I'll never have it; we'll take it."

Now there were two ladies with the money in their hot little hands saying, "I'll take it." And I was so broke that if ocean liners only cost fifty cents apiece, all I could do is stand on the sideline and say, "Ain't that cheap."

Let me ask you a couple of questions. If you were absolutely without any kind of funds at all, and two ladies are saying, "I'll take it," and you are working on a commission. If you had been the salesperson in that situation, what would you have done? Write the order, wouldn't you?

Guess what old Zig did? Scout's honor, I looked at my watch and said, "Ladies, I'd like nothing better in the world than to sell you that set of cookware, but I can't because I've got another appointment in just five minutes and I'm going to have to rush like crazy to get there."

With two ladies with their money in their hot little hands saying, "I'll take it," and I said, "Oh no, you won't. I've got something important to do." I actually left both of them sitting right there. Now anyone even on their dumbest, greenest day with enough gumption to get out of a telephone booth without written directions on the side—can you imagine anybody ever doing such a thing?

THERE'S ALWAYS HOPE

All I'm trying to say is, "Friend, there's hope for you!"

When I got to the appointment, the other prospect wasn't at home.

The next day I did make the sales from the night before. I wrote Mrs. Spence's order, but Mrs. Gates wasn't there. After I'd written Mrs. Spence's order, I said, "I thought Ms. Gates was going to be here." And that moment I saw her out the window and there she was running up the hill. She arrived all out of breath and said, "Oh, I was afraid you'd be gone again."

Some people have said that I may have been embellishing that story, but I'll absolutely guarantee you, I'm telling you to the best of my memory exactly like it happened. During those two and a half first years that I was in the business, I was a miserable producer, a miserable performer, a miserable human being. I was not happy with what I was doing. I tried to get other jobs, but when you're on a losing streak, most people simply do not want to hire you.

We were living in Lancaster, South Carolina at this time. There was an all-day meeting in Charlotte, North Carolina, and I went up there and spent the day and didn't learn anything. Now I might have learned something, but I long ago have forgotten what it was. I drove back home that night, had a demonstration, got in about 11:30 p.m. The baby kept us up most of the rest of the night. At 5:30

the next morning, the alarm clock sounded off to get me out of bed to go to the second day of the training school.

I rolled out of bed, I cracked the venetian blinds, looked out and did what any intelligent human being would do. I got back in bed. But as I lay down, the words of my mother came back to me, "Son, if you're in something get in it. If you're not in it, get out." When you say to somebody you're going to do something, you do it.

Now, when I had finally persuaded them to give me the job, I had promised them that I would always be present at sales meetings. I would always be present at training sessions; and though I had not done anything in my two and a half years, I had never missed a meeting. I had never even been late for a meeting. My mother's conditioning over all of those years rolled me out of bed. She had always said, "Son, when you're in something get in it. If you're not in it, get out." It is not fair to the person you're working for. You'll never make it with him or her. It is not being fair to yourself.

When you're in something get in it. If you're not in it, get out.

I drove those cold thirty-eight miles to Charlotte, North Carolina that day. The crowd was small. There were only about twenty people there. Mr. P.C. Merrill was conducting the session—he was my hero. He's the one who had written all of the training programs for the company. He is the one who set all of the records. He was the man everybody looked to in a very, very special way. He had a uniqueness about him, a wisdom about him that set him apart.

When the training session was over and again, I do not remember anything I learned at the session. But when it was all over, Mr. Merrill said, "Zig, I'd like you to stay behind. I need to talk with you a moment." It might be hard for you to really relate to this and appreciate it, but it absolutely thrilled me to death that Mr. Merrill wanted to talk to me. The little guy from the little town who was going to struggle all of his life.

Now don't misunderstand. My mother had always said to us that if you work hard, tell the truth, and love the Lord, everything will work out all right. But you see, I thought she meant I'd have something to eat, something to wear, and a place to sleep. That was the image that I had in those Depression years. Mr. Merrill now is saying, "I want to talk to you." I don't know whether it was by accident or design, but somehow or another I ended up in a corner and he was in front. The whole conversation probably lasted no more than two minutes.

He opened by saying, "As I've watched you for the last two and a half years, I have never seen such a waste." A comment like that will get your attention.

And I said, "Well, Mr. Merrill, what do you mean?"

YOU CAN BE A CHAMPION

He said, "Zig, I believe that you could be a great one. I believe you can be a national champion. I believe you could go to the very top in this company. And I believe that someday if you so elected to do so, you could even become an executive in this company—if you just went to work on a regular schedule and if you really recognized your own ability."

Please understand that from the first day, everybody had said go to work on a regular schedule. But when you're a little guy from a little town and you're going to struggle all of your life and you're never really going to amount to anything other than just being a provider for your needs, and somebody says, "go to work on a regular schedule," the natural tendency to ask, "Why? Why should I get out there and beat my head against the wall? Nothing good is going to come of it. Just look at me. I'm not a loser but I'm certainly not a winner. I'm just the little guy from the little town."

When you say to a youngster with a poor self-image, "stay away from drugs, they'll kill you," their natural reaction, if they have a poor self-image, is to think, *Don't tell me that. My friends tell me drugs make you feel good. They make you feel big. They make you part of the group. Besides, if they do hurt me, no big deal. There's nothing lost because I'm a nothing. I'm a nobody.*

Or if you say to a youngster with a poor self-image, "obey the law and study your lessons," they frequently think to themselves, *Why should I go through all that jazz? The rich kids are going get all the big breaks. I'm from the wrong side of the tracks. Nothing good is going to happen to me. Besides, if I don't make it, no big deal. I'll just be on welfare.*

When you say to the youngster with a poor self-image, "save yourself for the one you love until you're married," they frequently think, *Why should I do that? I want to have some fun now because I'm nothing and all of the desirable people are all going to be gone when I get ready to get married anyhow.*

But when you say to the youngster with the good self-image, "here are the facts about you," and then you tell him or her how unique and special and loved they are and how their future is bright and beautiful—they will believe it.

Mr. Merrill said to me, "Zig, you could be a national champion." I've thought about his comment so many times. What would my life have been like had Mr. Merrill been the wrong kind of man? What do I mean by that? If I had thought that Mr. Merrill was trying to get me jacked up so I'd go sell more cookware so he'd look good, his words would have had no meaning at all to me.

But friend, it's a basic fact of life. If people like you, they'll listen to you. If they trust you, they'll do what you request. They'll take action, which is in your best interests. Mr. Merrill said I could be a national champion and I believed him because his entire career had been built on honesty and character and integrity and trust and love and loyalty. My hero said, "You could be a national champion," and in my mind's eye, that's exactly what I saw.

Now I want to emphasize one critically important point. I had been taught by my friend Bill Cranford how to get prospects, how to put on demonstrations, how to handle objections, how to close sales. I was by then a trained salesperson. The salesman was ready.

Mr. Merrill got the person ready.

On the way home, that little Crosley automobile never touched the ground. What a marvelous trip it was.

I had three prospects at the demonstration that evening. They never had a chance. Had they been even half smart, they would have come in and said, "Okay, now Zig, we know there's no point in you going through the whole demonstration. We're going to buy. We know that already. Just give us some food, let us eat it, we'll sign up, and we can go home early." They were no longer dealing with the little guy from a little town who had struggled all of his life. They were now dealing with a national champion.

THE WAY YOU SEE YOURSELF

Let me say it again. *You cannot perform in a manner that is inconsistent with the way you see yourself.* In my mind, I was a national champion and that's the way I was acting.

I didn't quite make it as a national champion, but I did finish second in our sales organization of over 7,000. I swapped that little Crosley for a luxury car. I had the best promotion the company had to offer. The next year I was the highest paid person in the United States with that company, and three years later became the youngest divisional supervisor in the 66-year history of that company and set some records that still stand to this day.

Whether I speak for a group of 175 or whether it's for a group of 22,000 in Kansas City where I addressed FFA on more than one occasion, or whether it's to 16,000 people in an open seminar in Minneapolis, or for a dozen retired Baptist preachers—I never speak until I first have asked God to make me a P.C. Merrill in your life.

If there's anything I don't like about what I do, it's the fact that I never really get to know anyone very well. You've read this entire book, but I don't know you. We have the three-day Born to Win conferences and I see people for three days there. But the reality is, I have said, "Hello, how are you?" I have shaken some hands, though not all of them. I've exchanged a couple of pleasantries with two or three, but I've only had a matter of one second, five seconds, ten seconds. I don't really know the people I meet.

I've often wondered what it would be like if I had the privilege of spending time with everyone who has ever read one of my books, sat in one of my audiences, seen one of my videos, or heard one of the audio recordings. I wonder what it would be like.

I wish I could, but that doesn't seem to be possible. Today I'm in Dallas, tomorrow again I'll be speaking in Dallas, the next day I'll be speaking in Saint Louis. The next day I'll be back here and the story goes on like that and I never really get to know the people with whom I deal.

If you and I had some time together, what a privilege it would be for me to spend that time with you. Looking you right in the eye *I would say to you that you were designed for accomplishment. You're engineered for success. You're endowed with the seeds of greatness.* I would remind you that since the beginning of time, there have been over 11 billion people to walk the face of this earth, but there never has been and *there never will be another one just like you. You are rare. You're unique. You're different. You're a natural champion.*

THE MOST IMPORTANT VOTE

I don't know if you follow the political arena. I'm fascinated by it and I always have been. When the next election comes up, I so badly hope that you are registered to vote. And then I hope you register in the next one and the next one and the next one because if you don't take part in the political process, then you surrender all griping rights. You have no right to complain about anything that goes on here because you're not participating in the process. I hope you'll vote in future elections.

But I'm going to urge you at this moment to participate in the most important election you will ever vote in.

I'm going to ask you at this moment to step back into the polling booth of your own mind. And because this election is so enormously important, I'm going to suggest that you close the drapes so no one else can see your innermost thoughts and exactly how you're going to vote.

And as you step into this polling booth, if you will turn around, you will notice there's a series of levers up there for the people you can vote for. One of them stands out because the name is emblazoned in pure gold. That name is your very own.

I'm going to ask you to reach up, grab that lever vigorously, and forcefully pull down a vote for you. When you do, you will see that long ago, God had already voted for you. With those two votes, you can win any election or any contest you will ever enter as long as you live. That eternal arithmetic clearly says *you plus God equals enough.*

About
the Author

Zig Ziglar (1926-2012) was one of America's most influential and beloved encouragers and believers that everyone could be, do, and have more. He was a motivational speaker, teacher, and trainer who traveled extensively delivering messages of humor, hope, and encouragement. His appeal transcended age, culture, and occupation. From 1970 until 2010, Zig traveled more than five million miles around the world sharing powerful life-improvement messages, cultivating the energy of change.

Zig Ziglar wrote more than thirty celebrated books on personal growth, leadership, sales, faith, family, and success. He was a committed family man, dedicated patriot, and an active church member. His unique delivery style and powerful presentations earned him many honors, and today he is still considered one of the most versatile authorities on the science of human potential.